Cambridge Elements ≡

Elements in Perception
edited by
James T. Enns
The University of British Columbia

EMPATHY

From Perception to Understanding and Feeling Others' Emotions

Shir Genzer
Hebrew University of Jerusalem
Yoad Ben Adiva
Hebrew University of Jerusalem
Anat Perry
Hebrew University of Jerusalem

CAMBRIDGE
UNIVERSITY PRESS

Shaftesbury Road, Cambridge CB2 8EA, United Kingdom

One Liberty Plaza, 20th Floor, New York, NY 10006, USA

477 Williamstown Road, Port Melbourne, VIC 3207, Australia

314–321, 3rd Floor, Plot 3, Splendor Forum, Jasola District Centre,
New Delhi – 110025, India

103 Penang Road, #05–06/07, Visioncrest Commercial, Singapore 238467

Cambridge University Press is part of Cambridge University Press & Assessment,
a department of the University of Cambridge.

We share the University's mission to contribute to society through the pursuit of
education, learning and research at the highest international levels of excellence.

www.cambridge.org
Information on this title: www.cambridge.org/9781009454148

DOI: 10.1017/9781009281072

First published 2023

A catalogue record for this publication is available from the British Library

ISBN 978-1-009-45414-8 Hardback
ISBN 978-1-009-28110-2 Paperback
ISSN 2515-0502 (online)
ISSN 2515-0499 (print)

Cambridge University Press & Assessment has no responsibility for the persistence
or accuracy of URLs for external or third-party internet websites referred to in this
publication and does not guarantee that any content on such websites is, or will
remain, accurate or appropriate.

Empathy

From Perception to Understanding and Feeling Others' Emotions

Elements in Perception

DOI: 10.1017/9781009281072
First published online: November 2023

Shir Genzer
Hebrew University of Jerusalem

Yoad Ben Adiva
Hebrew University of Jerusalem

Anat Perry
Hebrew University of Jerusalem

Author for correspondence: Anat Perry, anat.perry@mail.huji.ac.il

Abstract: Empathy provides a cognitive and emotional bridge that connects individuals and promotes prosocial behavior. People empathize with others via two complementary perceptual routes: cognitive empathy or the ability to accurately recognize and understand others' emotional states, and affective empathy or the ability to "feel with" others. This Element reviews past and current research on both cognitive and affective empathy, focusing on behavioral, as well as neuroscientific research. It highlights a recent shift toward more dynamic and complex stimuli which may better capture the nature of real social interaction. It expands on why context is crucial when perceiving others' emotional state, and discusses gender differences, biases affecting our understanding of others, and perception of others in clinical conditions. Lastly, it highlights proposed future directions in the field.

Keywords: empathy, cognitive empathy, affective empathy, understanding others, social interactions

ISBNs: 9781009454148 (HB), 9781009281102 (PB), 9781009281072 (OC)
ISSNs: 2515-0502 (online), 2515-0499 (print)

Contents

1 Introduction

Empathy, our ability to similarly feel and comprehend the emotional states of others, is an essential and integral part of daily life. It helps us understand and identify with other people, create and maintain close relationships, and importantly increase prosocial behavior (Batson, 1991; de Waal, 2008; Eisenberg & Fabes, 1990; Lehmann et al., 2022).

Perception is a prerequisite for empathy. How we perceive the other's state affects how we understand the situation and what we feel. For example, imagine seeing a crying woman hugging her soldier husband in two scenarios: In one, they are at an airport after the husband returned home from a long deployment abroad, and in the other, they are in a cemetery during a funeral. The way we interpret the situation, how we feel toward the protagonists, and how we understand their emotional state all depend on our perception of the context. In the first scenario, one can infer that the woman is crying from overwhelming joy, happiness, and even relief for reuniting with her husband, whereas in the other scenario, she is crying from agonizing grief, pain, and sorrow for losing someone close to her.

How we perceive the situation clearly affects our empathy, and our empathy affects our perception. For example, various biases – such as whether we are listening to someone similar to or different from us – may affect how much we "feel with" that person. Our empathy, in turn, affects how we perceive the situation, how much pain we attribute to the other person, and how much we are willing to help them. Perceiving, understanding, and feeling the emotional states of others are thus intertwined, and will be the focus of the current Element.

Empathy is a multifaceted concept that has been defined in various ways in the literature (Hall & Schwartz, 2019). A commonly used conceptualization of empathy defines it as comprised of three main components (Zaki & Ochsner, 2012). The first is *cognitive empathy* (also known as mentalizing), which is the ability to recognize and understand others' emotions and feelings. The second component is *affective empathy* (also known as emotional empathy or experience sharing), which is the ability to share others' emotions or "feel with" them while maintaining the distinction between self and other (Abramson et al., 2020; Jolliffe & Farrington, 2004; Zaki & Ochsner, 2012). Although most researchers have studied these two components separately, recent evidence from naturalistic tasks and neuroimaging studies indicates that in real social interaction these two components often operate together and affect one another (for meta-analysis and integrative review, see Schurz et al., 2021). *Motivational empathy* (also known as empathic care) is another important component. Motivation plays a crucial role in facilitating empathic processes and consequent prosocial behavior (Cameron et al., 2019; Zaki, 2014). Although we may possess the ability to empathize, researchers have shown that the act of empathizing is costly and without proper motivation, individuals often tend to avoid it (Cameron et al., 2019; Feruguson et al., 2020). Moreover, some clinical conditions show a distinction between the ability to empathize and having a propensity to actually empathize (Keysers & Gazzola, 2014). While motivational factors are important to take into account and will be mentioned sporadically throughout this Element, we take a perception-focused view of empathy and so will expand more on the first two components.

The following sections expand on each of these two components, cognitive and affective empathy, highlighting what is currently known about how we understand and share the experiences of others. We then devote a section to brain networks enabling empathy, expand on why context is crucial when perceiving others' emotional state, and discuss gender differences, biases affecting our understanding of others, and perception of others in clinical conditions. We conclude by highlighting future directions in the field.

2 Cognitive Empathy

Cognitive empathy (also known as mentalizing) refers to the ability to recognize and understand others' emotions and feelings (Uzefovsky & Knafo-Noam, 2016). We distinguish cognitive empathy from related concepts such as perspective-taking and Theory of Mind. The two latter terms refer to more general processes of understanding others' thoughts, beliefs, and intentions and not just their emotions and feelings (Byom & Mutlu, 2013; Cuff et al., 2016); they are therefore beyond the scope of this Element. We next describe how different factors such as information cues, knowledge, and feedback affect our perception and therefore influence how we interpret others' emotional state. In addition, we discuss recent changes in the way researchers experimentally test these concepts and questions in the lab.

2.1 The Roles of Different Information Cues

To better understand how perception affects and shapes our ability to recognize and relate to others' emotional states, it is essential to consider which cues incorporate socially relevant information about others' feelings. According to the basic emotion account, emotional facial and vocal expressions convey specific emotions that are recognized universally (Keltner et al., 2019; Sauter et al., 2015; Sauter, Eisner, Ekman, et al., 2010). This implies a simple and direct link between a perceived facial or vocal expression and a specific interpretation of the other's emotions. Conversely, the dimensional account suggests that emotional facial and vocal expressions could be clear indicators of affective properties of valence (positivity or negativity) but not for specific emotions, which are culturally variable (Gendron et al., 2014; Jack et al., 2012; Marsella & Gratch, 2014). The cultural variability in identifying specific emotions implies that our cultural background shapes how we perceive and interpret emotional expressions (see also Section 8.2, Individual and Cultural Differences). Finally, a growing body of evidence reinforces a functional-contextual view, which highlights the role of context in emotion recognition. According to the functional-contextual theory, emotional facial and vocal expressions do not necessarily express unique and unambiguous emotions or affect, and their meaning is often context-dependent (Atias et al., 2019; Aviezer et al., 2017; Barrett et al., 2011; Crivelli & Fridlund, 2018). Indeed, in a study investigating whether people integrate information from faces and situations (i.e., the contextual information) to infer others' emotions, a Bayesian model based on situation information alone predicted people's inference about emotions better than a Bayesian cue-integration model, indicating the importance of contextual information for the perception and interpretation of facial expressions (Goel et al., 2022). Similarly, in a study that used real videos (e.g., of families reuniting with a homecoming soldier), facial expressions alone were rated as negative and failed to convey diagnostic information about the positive situational valence. However, when contextual information appeared alone or with the face, participants accurately rated the target as feeling positive. These findings demonstrate the vital role of contextual information in emotion perception from facial expressions in real-life situations (Israelashvili et al., 2019).

As previously mentioned, the conveyed message encompasses not only facial expressions but also auditory information including vocalizations (e.g., gasps, screams, or sighs; Cordaro et al., 2016; Hawk et al., 2009; Sauter, Eisner, Ekman, et al., 2010) and paralinguistic vocal cues (e.g., pitch, cadence, speed, volume, prosody, and intensity; Banse & Scherer, 1996; Laukka et al., 2016) that convey vital affective information on emotional states (Lange et al., 2022; Patel et al., 2011; Sauter, Eisner, Calder, et al., 2010; Sundberg et al., 2011). Indeed, whenever we speak or vocalize, we convey both the meaning contained in the words we choose and rich nonverbal information on our emotional state through paralinguistic vocal cues and nonlinguistic vocalizations (Laukka & Elfenbein, 2021). Numerous computational models have been used to predict emotions from paralinguistic vocal cues, reinforcing the notion that these cues convey vital information about the speaker's emotions (for a review, see Wang et al., 2022).

As emphasized earlier, the interpretation of vocalizations is not always straightforward, and similar to vision, could be highly dependent on the context in which the vocalization is produced. For instance, Atias and colleagues (2019) demonstrated that vocalizations from both highly positive and negative situations are perceived as negative when presented alone. When the vocalizations were presented with contextual visual information, perceptions mainly depended on the contextual information, such that the same vocalizations sounded positive or negative when paired with a differently valenced visual context.

Verbal, linguistic, and semantic content are, of course, other central components in human communication that could carry direct or concealed information on others' emotional states. Several studies investigated this question in the setting of therapy sessions. These studies focus on the therapist's language as a predictor of the therapist's empathy, stressing the critical role language plays in the quality of psychotherapy (Gibson et al., 2015; Xiao et al., 2012). Hall and Schmid (2007) explored the impact of semantic information beyond the context of therapy using the empathic accuracy task. Participants were asked to watch videos of people sharing autobiographical stories and rate their feelings (for more details on empathic accuracy, see Section 2.2, Empathic Accuracy). To investigate the role of verbal and semantic information in an accurate understanding of the other's feelings, the videos were presented under four conditions: full video, audio, transcript, and silent video. The results indicated that verbal information contributed the most to accuracy. However, a significant difference between the audio and the transcript conditions indicates that vocal nonverbal cues improve accuracy (Hall & Schmid, 2007). Computational modeling has also been extensively used to investigate the role of verbal and linguistic content as a carrier of emotional information. Yoon and colleagues (2018) have found that a model which simultaneously utilizes information from audio and text sequences from speech for recognizing emotions, results in higher accuracy than previous models that focus only on audio features. This result implies that verbal content holds additional information on the other's emotions compared to the information obtained from the auditory channel alone (Yoon et al., 2018; for more information, see review by Wang et al., 2022). Finally, the increased use of digital communication spurred a growing body of research investigating emotion recognition from textual paralinguistic cues such as emojis or emoticons (:-D), character repetitions (*yeeei*), and nonstandard or multiple punctuations (*!!!, #%#!!*; see Rodríguez-Hidalgo et al., 2017), or even from typos in emails (Blunden & Brodsky, 2021).

2.2 Empathic Accuracy

Empathic accuracy refers to one's ability to draw an accurate inference about the other's emotional state. Most previous research that investigated how accurate people are at inferring other's emotions, either used self-report questionnaires (Davis, 1983; De Corte et al., 2007; Spreng et al., 2009), or recognition tasks with still images (Aviezer et al., 2008; Ekman et al., 1972; Naor et al., 2018), eyes depicting emotions (Reading the Mind in the Eyes Task; Baron-Cohen et al., 2001), or short videos of actors (Atkinson et al., 2004; Yitzhak et al., 2020). While there is great value in studying basic communication skills in isolation, using well-controlled, easily replicable stimuli in the lab, there are also downsides to these designs. First and foremost, we do not know how the targets in these pictures actually felt. Second, they lack ecological validity; that is, they do not convey the complexity of everyday interactions nor the naturalistic and dynamic nature of real social interactions. Moreover, by using unimodal, simplified stimuli, we could miss the holistic and additive effects that arise from the integration of various sources of information in the process of understanding others' emotional states. In most cases, these simplified stimuli also lack the contextual information in which the emotional expressions have occurred, limiting an observer's ability to recognize emotions as is done "in the wild." Furthermore, participants are often required to assess an emotional expression with a singular response, which is compared to one "correct" answer (Rum & Perry, 2020). By that, an assumption is being made that the specific emotional facial or vocal expression conveys a unique and distinct singular emotion. Moreover, these settings mostly disregard the possibility of simultaneously feeling and expressing multiple emotions.

In recent years, social psychologists and neuroscientists called for finding more naturalistic ways to study empathic accuracy in the lab (Osborne-Crowley, 2020; Watt, 2014). In the next section, we describe in detail one such set of tasks, the empathic accuracy (EA) tasks. Empathic accuracy tasks refer to similar but different paradigms that attempt to overcome the limitations previously described. They use a more naturalistic setting that better captures the dynamic and complex nature of real social interaction and combines different information channels instead of focusing solely on one modality. Most importantly, they have a "ground truth" of people's reported emotional states, which can then be compared to the observer's evaluation. It should be noted that the tasks, being naturalistic in nature, require not only cognitive empathy abilities but also involve affective empathy, and that these are often intertwined and affect each other (Genzer et al., 2022; Sened et al., 2020; Zaki & Ochsner, 2011).

In the original task, which was developed by Ickes and colleagues (1990), dyads were videotaped interacting with one another. In the next step, both dyad members were asked to view the videotape and pause at each point when they remembered having had a specific thought or feeling and write it down, so each dyad's member made a written, time-logged listing of the actual thoughts/ feelings. The dyad members were then instructed to view the videotape a second time, with stops at times at which their interaction partner reported a thought or feeling. For each time point, the other was asked to provide an inference (in writing) regarding the content of their partner's thoughts and feelings. Empathic accuracy is operationalized as the similarity between the target self-reported thought/feeling and the one inferred by the perceiver, as assessed by judges. This design allows researchers to investigate the understanding of emotional states in naturalistic conversation. Each participant freely chooses when to report thoughts/feelings and which word to use to describe them without limiting the number of thoughts/feelings that can be given for each time point. This setting prevents an anchoring effect that could occur when participants are asked to select emotions from options offered by a researcher. However, the estimated EA scores from this design are strongly dependent on judges' evaluation and, therefore, could be less objective and more prone to biases and differences between various studies and judges.

Another way to measure EA in couples over longer time periods than one conversation is through daily diaries. In this design, participants provide regular reports of their own and their partner's current emotions over several days or weeks. By comparing the partners' ratings, EA scores can be calculated (Howland & Rafaeli, 2010; Sened et al., 2017). This design facilitates the assessment of the capacity to understand others' emotions and feelings outside the lab and is therefore considered to be more naturalistic. It also could be used to evaluate how different relationship factors affect understanding of emotions over time, and not just during a single interaction. On the other hand, this design is limited to people who have close relationships with daily interactions, and hence it mainly applies to a narrower range of relationship types. Moreover, because each dyad rates a different set of events, this could lead to unknown confounds; and each dyad's uniqueness ensures that no two people see and rate the same person. Therefore it is difficult to know whether differences between raters can be attributed to differences in trait empathy, in understanding one's specific partner, or to the interaction.

Finally, in a third approach, which was developed by Levenson and Ruef (1992), married couples were videotaped while conversing with one another on both "events of the day," and a conflictive problem area in their marriage. Several days later, each partner returned to the laboratory, watched their videos and provided continuous ratings on how they felt at each moment. These videos can be shown to new participants ("perceivers") who are asked to infer and rate the affect of the partners in a similar way. Again, EA is operationalized as the correspondence between the perceiver's and the partners' ratings (for more details, see Allison & Liker 1982; Levenson & Gottman, 1983; Levenson & Ruef, 1992). Zaki and colleagues (2008) later used a similar paradigm, but instead of videotaped conversations between married couples, they videotaped participants ("storytellers") while sharing emotional autobiographical stories from their lives (for modifications of this task and additions of physiological measurements of both storyteller and perceiver, see Jospe et al., 2020). This design enables us to parametrically evaluate the emotional change as well as the accuracy change over time. Moreover, the balance between the naturalistic and controlled nature of the design allows us to examine the complex and dynamic process of understanding emotions, while also manipulating different aspects of the stimuli and presenting them to a large number of people. For instance, we can use these naturalistic videos (which include both facial expressions and auditory information) to assess the contributions of different information channels separately (see Figure 1).

Indeed, several studies showed that at least in short (two to three minutes) emotional communication with a stranger, the auditory channel and most likely the verbal and linguistic information play crucial roles in understanding the emotional state of the storyteller. While the average person fares better than

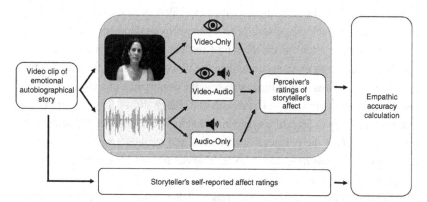

Figure 1 An example of an empathic accuracy task (adapted from Genzer et al., 2022). Participants view multiple video clips of autobiographical stories in three viewing conditions: Video-Only (without audio), Video-Audio, and Audio-Only (without video). Throughout the story, they are asked to rate how they think the storyteller felt. Based on the correlation between these ratings and those of the storyteller, an empathic accuracy score can be calculated.

chance at inferring another's emotions from a video alone, the visual channel does not add much once you can hear the other person (Genzer et al., 2022; Gesn & Ickes, 1999; Hall & Schmid Mast, 2007; Jospe et al., 2020, 2022). Note that in this paradigm, there is no live interaction, no accumulating knowledge (beyond the two-minute video), and no partner to get feedback from on how well you understood them.

2.3 The Importance of Accumulating Knowledge and Feedback

From the beginning of an acquaintance with a person, we receive direct or indirect feedback on how well we understand them. This feedback is essential to modify how we perceive and interpret the other's unique nuances and cues for effective communication. The importance of accumulating knowledge and feedback was demonstrated in a clinical setting, revealing that, on average, empathic accuracy of the perceiver improved with increased exposure to the target, and that feedback regarding the target's actual emotions, accelerated this process (Marangoni et al., 1995; see also Barone et al., 2005 and Lobchuk et al., 2016 for similar results with psychology students viewing clinical sessions, and with nursing students discussing health risk behaviors with a caregiver). The advantage of giving feedback, versus other practices, was demonstrated in a recent study (Israelashvili & Perry, 2021) in which participants watched several videos of a target sharing his or her experiences. Participants were randomly assigned to the Feedback condition in which, after rating the target's emotions in a specific video, they received information on how the target actually felt before they continued to the next video; or to the control condition in which no feedback was given; or to a perspective-taking condition in which participants were asked to do their best to "get into the other's shoes." The Feedback group was more accurate than the two other groups at understanding the target's emotions across time, stressing the importance of sharing emotions and accumulating knowledge (Israelashvili & Perry, 2021). This research adds to a growing body of literature suggesting that it is quite difficult and sometimes impossible to *take* the perspective of others, and implies instead that the goal can be to *get perspective*, that is, to learn about the other's emotional state by asking for more information (Eyal et al., 2018).

Other studies of dyadic interaction reported that close friends achieved higher empathic accuracy than strangers (Stinson & Ickes, 1992), and that dating partners were significantly more accurate than both friends and strangers (Thomas & Fletcher, 2003), implying that both amount of time and relationship quality are key factors in the ability to understand the other.

3 Affective Empathy

The previous section focused on the more cognitive aspects of the empathic process. Relatedly, affective empathy (also known as *experience sharing*) is best understood as feeling with others, or having a similar emotional response to another's perceived emotional state (Hall & Schwartz, 2019; Marsh, 2022). For instance, consider the story about the sobbing woman in the cemetery from the previous example as described in Section 1. Perceiving her emotional reaction to losing someone close to her can lead us to feel a similar negative emotion ourselves and to share her emotional state. Note that while some researchers define affective empathy as experiencing the exact same emotion as the target (she feels devastated, I feel devastated), others take a more general view and extend affective empathy to include similar emotional responses that are triggered by the emotional state of the target (she feels devastated, I feel sad or worried; Murphy et al., 2022). When the emotional response is not identical to that of the target, some may define it as compassion.

To grasp the concept of affective empathy it is important to note some related but distinct terms: *emotional contagion, compassion* and *personal distress*. *Emotional contagion* refers to feeling what the other is feeling but in contrast to our view of affective empathy, does not include a self-other distinction – a key element of empathic processes that involves identifying that the other's emotional state is the source of one's own emotional state. Affective empathy includes emotional sharing, while maintaining a self-other distinction (Bird & Viding, 2014; Lamm et al., 2016; Zaki & Ochsner, 2012). The two other terms, compassion and personal distress, incorporate motivational approach/avoidance factors. *Compassion* (also referred to as empathic concern) is an other-oriented response, characterized by feeling warmth and concern for others, which produces altruistic approach motivations and is believed to serve as a catalyst of prosocial behavior (Batson et al., 2015). Affective empathy, in addition to inducing compassionate and prosocial responses, may lead to *personal distress*, a self-oriented aversive response to others' emotional state that produces an egoistic motivation to reduce own aversive arousal and may lead to avoidance and reduce the probability of subsequent prosocial behavior (FeldmanHall et al., 2015; Preckel et al., 2018; Singer & Klimecki, 2014). In this Element, we consider affective empathy as a more general term, referring to a process of sharing others' experience, regardless of the underling motivational factors. The following section addresses the challenges of measuring affective empathy and then focuses on one prominent design commonly used in affective empathy research, that of empathy for pain. Lastly, we review how contextual factors can affect affective empathy.

3.1 Measuring Affective Empathy

Measuring affective empathy is a challenging and arduous task, tapping into "how much" we feel with or for others. A vast range of methods aims to capture this complex ability, varying in conceptualization, objectivity, and how well they simulate real-world social interaction.

One type of measure is based on individual subjective reports, assessing one's trait, state, or emotional resonance with others. Trait affective empathy is usually measured by self-report questionnaires probing an individual's subjective dispositional tendency to share or react to another's emotional state (e.g., "I tend to get emotionally involved with a friend's problems"; Baron-Cohen & Wheelwright, 2004; Davis, 1983; for a review, see Neumann et al., 2015). Emotional reactivity state measures are assessed by self-report ratings of the individual's emotional response to perceiving different emotional cues in others – for instance, rating the amount of unpleasantness or distress felt while perceiving someone else in pain (Fan & Han, 2008; Lamm et al., 2007; Rainville et al., 1997). Affective empathy can also be measured by asking both a target and a perceiver what they each felt when the target was in some form of distress. The congruency between target and perceiver's self-reported emotional-state ratings (similar to the empathic accuracy task described in Section 2.2, Empathic Accuracy) could be described as "experience sharing" or affective empathy. Whereas higher unpleasantness ratings may represent a perceiver's greater sensitivity, lower threshold, or a general tendency to exaggerate, this congruency measure aligns more with the conceptualization of affective empathy as dependent on the target's emotional state, and it evaluates how well one "matches" with the other's emotions (Coll et al., 2017).

Other measures are indirect, implicit methods, assessing physiological responses to emotional stimuli. These responses can represent emotional reactivity and arousal, as in the case of psychophysiological reactions (Neumann & Westbury, 2011). Perceiving emotional cues can provoke different physiological patterns indicating an emotional response, evident in cardiovascular activity (Palomba et al., 2000), skin conductance (Banks et al., 2012; Fusaro et al., 2016; Hein et al., 2011), respiratory rate (Gomez et al., 2004), facial electromyography (Sato et al., 2008), a combination of these different indicators (Aguado et al., 2018; Bernat et al., 2006; Britton et al., 2006; Brouwer et al., 2013; Gantiva et al., 2021; Kreibig et al., 2007), and more (Kosonogov et al., 2017; for a review see Kreibig, 2010). Physiological activation (including neural activity) is sometimes interpreted as underlying shared representations. According to the simulation theory (Goldman, 2006), perceiving or even merely imagining another's emotional state activates similar psychological, physiological, and neural processes as the first-hand emotional experience. This simulation or *interpersonal resonance* is thought to facilitate a representation of others' affective states in ourselves (i.e., sharing others' emotional experiences; Bastiaansen et al., 2009; de Waal & Preston, 2017; Decety & Jackson, 2004; Preston & de Waal, 2002; Singer et al., 2004). This contributes to our ability to understand others' feelings and intentions, and promotes prosocial motivation and consequent behavior (de Vignemont & Singer, 2006; de Waal & Preston, 2017; Preston & de Waal, 2002; Zaki & Ochsner, 2012). However, note that evidence is still limited regarding the exact role of physiological responses in the empathic process (Deuter et al., 2018) or in prosocial behavior (Hein et al., 2011), and these relationships are still being studied and debated.

Another way to use physiological measures to try to tap affective empathy processes indirectly is to look at the physiological synchrony between the two partners. For example, in a recent study, Chen and colleagues (2021) measured the physiological activation (heart rate, skin conductance, and finger pulse amplitude) of couples while they were engaging in a conversation on different topics. A few days later, the couples returned to the lab to separately watch videos of their conversations while continuously rating how they each felt. This enabled assessing both physiological and affective synchrony between partners as well as the connection between the couple's physiological and affective synchrony. The study revealed greater physiological synchrony between partners when sharing positive emotions. Physiological synchrony between dyads has also been associated with higher-quality interactions and relationships (Chen et al., 2021; Feldman et al., 2011; for a review see Mayo et al., 2021; Palumbo et al., 2017; Timmons et al., 2015), health and longevity (Wells et al., 2022), it has been shown to correlate with both negative and positive shared emotional experience (Chen et al., 2021; Dor-Ziderman et al., 2021; Feldman et al., 2011; Goldstein et al., 2017; Golland et al., 2015) and with other empathic capacities (Chatel-Goldman et al., 2014; Jospe et al., 2020; Levenson & Ruef, 1992; Soto & Levenson, 2009).

In similar fashion, physiological synchrony can also be measured between brains. Inter-brain synchrony can be assessed through the congruency between a perceiver's and a target's neural activity obtained by hyperscanning, which simultaneously measures neural responses (or proxies thereof) from two or more participants via functional magnetic resonance imaging (fMRI), electro-encephalography (EEG), magnetoencephalography (MEG) or functional near infrared spectroscopy (fNIRS; Czeszumski et al., 2020, 2022; Wang et al., 2018). Inter-brain synchrony research is in its early stages, and what cognitive purpose it serves is still under debate (Dumas et al., 2010; Hasson et al., 2012;

Liu et al., 2018). It was previously connected to successful verbal and nonverbal communication (Hasson et al., 2012; Stephens et al., 2010), cooperative behavior (Hu et al., 2018; for a recent meta-analysis see Czeszumski et al., 2022), mother–child behavioral synchrony (Levy et al., 2017), communication of emotional cues (Anders et al., 2011), affective sharing (Nummenmaa et al., 2012; Peng et al., 2021), and other empathy-related capacities (Goldstein et al., 2018).

Yet another way to think about interpersonal resonance in the brain is to compare activation of neural networks associated with first-hand emotional experiences to those associated with perceiving them second-hand (perceiving another's emotional expressions). Evidence for overlapping activation has been previously found in various emotional and sensory states, such as feeling and observing others feel disgust (Wicker et al., 2003), reward (Morelli et al., 2015), embarrassment (Krach et al., 2011; Paulus et al., 2018), touch (Blakemore et al., 2005; Keysers et al., 2004), and most commonly in response to pain (Avenanti et al., 2005; Jackson et al., 2005; Lamm et al., 2007; Lamm et al., 2011, 2019; Morrison et al., 2004; Riečanský & Lamm, 2019; Singer et al., 2004; see next section for details).

Finally, it should be noted that while the variety of methods used to measure affective empathy (which were not all included in the current review) presents vast research opportunities and can be used to accumulate converging evidence (Hall & Schwartz, 2019; Neumann et al., 2015; Zaki & Ochsner, 2012), this diversity may create difficulties when trying to compare results (Lamm & Majdandžić, 2015; Zaki & Ochsner, 2012). Differences between measurements claiming to represent similar constructs are evident (Murphy & Lilienfeld, 2019) and can confuse inferences about each study's theoretical implications. To overcome this problem, research should avoid vague terms, be clear about what is measured, and use converging evidence from a combination of different measurement tools, together with similar research designs to that of past work.

3.2 Empathy for Pain

Seeing others in pain is a salient cue and a strong driver of empathy. The pain reaction of others conveys an essential social signal with immense evolutionary importance, which immediately provokes a physiological reaction (Bastian et al., 2014; Williams, 2002). For these reasons, pain can be easily and reliably operationalized in lab settings and has shown mostly consistent neural evidence for shared activation (Fallon et al., 2020; Lamm et al., 2011; Timmers et al., 2018). As a result, empathy for pain is a central theme in empathy literature in

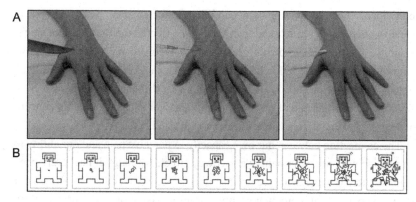

Figure 2 (A) Examples of stimuli used in empathy for pain tasks (unpublished, from Perry's lab). Participants are often asked to passively watch such pictures while in the scanner, or are asked to rate what they think the other is feeling, or what these pictures make them feel. From left to right: a hand being pricked by a knife, a hand pricked by a needle, a hand touched by a Q-tip (no pain); (B) A self-assessment manikin scale (SAM; Bradley & Lang, 1994), commonly used to assess nonverbal affective responses.

general, and more specifically when studying our tendency to share the emotional experiences of others (see Figure 2).

Our own pain perception and the capacity to feel other's pain are connected. Individual differences in pain sensitivity, measured by participant ratings of electrical stimulations (Li et al., 2020) or by the cold pressor test (which assesses participants' tolerance for keeping their hand in cold water; Ren et al., 2020), have been shown to correlate with trait empathy subjective self-report questionnaires, ratings of unpleasantness in response to painful stimuli, and empathy-related neural response (Li et al., 2020; Ren et al., 2020). Additional evidence for the connection between self-pain perception and shared pain can be found in studies conducted on clinical populations, such as people with congenital insensitivity to pain (CIP). Congenital insensitivity to pain is a rare condition in which patients cannot feel physical pain. Danziger and colleagues (2006) have found that patients with CIP, compared to healthy controls, show reduced aversive emotional response to pain-related stimuli. Interestingly, reduction of pain sensitivity by manipulation can affect empathy for others' pain also in the general population. Indeed, it was found that painkillers such as Acetaminophen (paracetamol) not only reduce our own pain, but also our ability to empathize with others' pain (Mischkowski et al., 2016). Furthermore, a series of studies demonstrated that perceivers' pain sensitivity can be manipulated simply by the belief that one has taken a painkiller. Inducing participants with placebo-analgesia (a placebo pill that participants believe to be a real painkiller) affected their pain response to electric nociceptive stimuli and, consequently, affected their ratings and neural response for perceiving others' pain as they received the same nociceptive stimuli (Rütgen et al., 2018; Rütgen, Seidel, Riečanský, et al., 2015; Rütgen, Seidel, Silani, et al., 2015). Administrating placebo-analgesia has also been found to affect subsequent motivation and behavior such as empathic concern and costly prosocial behavior (Hartmann et al., 2022).

The connection between our own capacity to perceive pain and our ability to empathize with others in pain is a two-way street. Although it has rarely been studied, there is some evidence for the effect of perceiving others in pain on our own pain perception. Perceiving a stranger telling an emotionally painful story while experiencing thermal stimulus was shown to increase participants' rating of intensity and unpleasantness of the painful stimulus (Loggia et al., 2008). A more recent study has shown that suboptimal exposure (priming) of injured limbs can increase ratings of pain intensity and unpleasantness for different painful stimuli (painful auditory and nociceptive stimuli; Ren et al., 2022).

3.3 Context Matters

Sharing or reacting to another's state is commonly considered an unconscious, stimuli-driven process whereby perception of others' emotional or sensory state generates a reflexive representation in the perceiver (de Waal & Preston, 2017; Decety & Jackson, 2004; Preston & de Waal, 2002; Singer & Lamm, 2009). A large number of studies in the field of empathy for pain use passive viewing tasks in which participants are shown pictures of injured limbs or a painful facial expression while their neural response is measured, emphasizing the automaticity of this process (Jackson et al., 2005; Schurz et al., 2021; see e.g., Figure 2). Yet the influence of social information and context on our capacity to share others' emotions are pervasive factors that can increase or inhibit our reaction to another's state (de Vignemont & Singer, 2006, Hoenen et al., 2013; Melloni et al., 2014; Singer & Lamm, 2009). Even low-intensity background, and unattended contextual cues can affect this process. For example, emotionally negative (e.g., sad) background music added to an emotional story can enhance our empathic response to others' distress (McDonald et al., 2022). Given that different sources of contextual information we perceive can influence our tendency to share another's state, we next focus on three major factors in this process: cue, target, and perceiver.

Differences in a cue's intensity can lead to a compatible modulation of the shared emotion intensity – for example, seeing others deeply penetrated by a needle rather than receiving a delicate pinprick can increase our response

(Avenanti et al., 2006; Hoenen et al., 2015; Saarela et al., 2007). Additional contextual information regarding the cue's realism and authenticity can modulate this effect. For example, watching cartoon-based cues in comparison to picture-based cues elicits lower emotional reaction in the perceiver (Fan & Han, 2008; Gu & Han, 2007). Likewise, how much we believe the other's pain to be genuine can affect our response, such that watching pain inflicted on an actor or a robot tends to result in a diminished empathic response (Suzuki et al., 2015; Wu & Han, 2021).

Our relationship with the individual in pain and our evaluation of the individual's traits and actions can have an immense effect on our tendency to share his or her emotions. Think of your reaction to hearing about or seeing your child or a friend being injured versus a stranger. Perceiving others as more "psychologically close" and as more similar to us can enhance our empathic response to their pain (Cheng et al., 2010; Grynberg & Konrath, 2020; Ionta et al., 2020; López-Solà et al., 2020; Preis & Kroener-Herwig, 2012). In contrast, seeing others as different from us can have an inverse effect, reducing our tendency to share their experience (see Section 6, Biases and Limitations of Empathy).

Social information about the target can also affect the processes of experience sharing. We tend to feel more empathy for the weak and poor than for the rich and strong. Perceiving others as having higher social status can reduce our empathic response to their pain (Feng et al., 2016). Jealousy derived from information about the other receiving monetary reward (Guo et al., 2012) or having an attractive partner (Zheng, Zhang, et al., 2016) may prevent us from feeling their pain. Moral evaluation and judgment of others' past actions can have a similar modulating effect. Perceiving others as unfair (Singer et al., 2006), immoral (Cui et al., 2016), threatening (Cui et al., 2017), and as having a bad reputation (Zheng, Wang, et al., 2016) can reduce our tendency to share their emotions. In contrast, seeing others' pain as deliberately caused by another has a reverse effect and enhances empathic response (Akitsuki & Decety, 2009).

The perceiver's traits, past experience, and relationship with the target have all been shown to affect the tendency to feel empathy with the other. In addition, the perceiver's own emotional and physiological state has a key role in how much empathy they feel. For instance, sleep deprivation has been shown to induce a more self-centered and socially withdrawn state (Ben-Simon & Walker, 2018), accompanied by impaired communication and understanding of other people (Holding et al., 2019). Sleep deprivation may also impair emotional perception, lead individuals to perceive other people's negative emotions as less intense (Tempesta et al., 2018; Kyle et al., 2014), and impair emotional reactions (Duan et al., 2021). This has immense implications in a society that is commonly sleep-deprived, and especially for workplaces that involve shiftwork and empathic decision-making, such as hospitals. Indeed, a recent study shows that following nightshifts, physicians experienced less empathy for pain, were less likely to prescribe analgesics (compared to daytime shifts), and prescribed fewer analgesics than generally recommended by the World Health Organization (Choshen-Hillel et al., 2022).

The perceiver's prior exposure and expertise can also modulate the empathic response. Prior exposure to violence (Guo et al., 2013) or pain (Preis et al., 2013) may cause habituation and impair one's tendency to share another's pain. Of particular interest to researchers studying empathy for pain are health-care workers, who are prone to sleep deprivation, are regularly exposed to patients in pain, and are often engaged as part of their work in inflicting painful procedures themselves. Cheng and colleagues (2007) showed acupuncture practitioners pictures of body parts with needles inserted. The acupuncture practitioners showed lower neural empathic-pain response and lower ratings of pain intensity and unpleasantness than did control participants (for a similar study using event-related potential see Decety, et al., 2010; for more on specific brain regions, see Section 4, Brain Networks Associated with Empathy).

Although these studies showed an effect of prior exposure and expertise on empathic response, it is important to note that these effects do not stand by themselves, and they can also be modulated by context and environment. In a more recent study Cheng and colleagues (2017) showed the effect of contextual information and environment on health-care workers' empathic responses to others' pain. Health-care workers were exposed to visual and semantic information regarding the context and environment with two different contexts (home or hospital), before being exposed to a picture of body parts in pain. After being primed with a home rather than work context, health-care workers showed greater activation of brain areas related to empathic pain (see Section 4, Brain Networks Associated with Empathy). This activation was correlated with participants' ratings of valence, but only in the home context. This study shows the various adjustments our cognitive system can make when perceiving and processing different contextual information in order to adapt us to our complex, demanding, and changing social environment. Note that health-care workers' regulated, or decreased, empathic response (sharing less of others' painful state) may sometimes have an adaptive advantage, representing reduced personal distress, a benefit for both doctors and patients. Reducing personal distress may free cognitive resources for reasoning, allow better understanding of the others' state, and reduce burnout (Decety, 2020; Israelashvili et al., 2020; Powell, 2018).

4 Brain Networks Associated with Empathy

The neural systems supporting empathy are a main focus of social-neuroscience research, resulting in numerous studies that used different techniques and tasks to investigate which neuronal activity is associated with empathy, broadly defined. Most studies assessing empathy-related brain activation have used fMRI, which relies on the blood-oxygen-level-dependent (BOLD) signal, reflecting changes in deoxyhemoglobin driven by localized changes in brain blood flow and blood oxygenation. This technique takes advantage of the assumption that cerebral blood flow is coupled to underlying neuronal activity, and thus serves as a proxy for task-relevant brain activation (Hillman, 2014; Logothetis, 2008; Logothetis et al., 2001).

Since each study used different paradigms and usually a rather small number of participants, results on the neural underpinnings of empathy vary, but there are some common regions that emerge. In meta-analyses of fMRI studies that used cognitive/affective definitions of empathy similar to those in the current Element, empathy's affective and cognitive components were found to activate different regions, as well as a set of conserved areas. Cognitive empathy has been associated with frontal activation, for example, in the orbitofrontal cortex (OFC), ventromedial prefrontal cortex (vmPFC) and dorsomedial prefrontal gyrus (dmPFG), as well as the temporoparietal junction (TPJ), the precuneus, and the supramarginal gyrus (SMG), among other regions. Affective empathy has been associated with activation mostly in the anterior insula (AI), anterior midcingulate cortex (aMCC), inferior frontal gyrus (IFG), midbrain, and supplementary motor area (SMA) (Fan et al., 2011; Kogler et al., 2020; Timmers et al., 2018). Some brain regions were found to be associated with both cognitive and affective components of empathy. These include the dorsal anterior cingulate cortex (dACC), aMCC, SMA, and AI or the dorsal medial thalamus (DMT) suggesting a common core network, perhaps relating to broader social-cognitive processes (Fan et al., 2011; Timmers et al., 2018).

Importantly, most neuroimaging studies have used simplified stimuli (e.g., still pictures of hands experiencing pain), since they are easier to control and repeat in repeated-measures designs. Moreover, earlier work did not correlate brain activation with actual behavior (Zaki & Ochsner, 2012), limiting our interpretation of the neuroimaging results. In a study that attempted to address these limitations, the empathic accuracy paradigm described in Section 2.2 was used while brain activity was recorded via fMRI (Zaki et al., 2009). The authors' main goal was to uncover whether the more cognitive network or the affective one (there referred to as mental state attributions network versus the shared representations network) is more important for empathic accuracy.

Their results led to the conclusion that both are important. Empathic accuracy performance was predicted by activity in the dorsal and rostral subregions of the MPFC and the superior temporal sulcus – regions that are considered part of a perceiver's mental state attributions brain network – and also by activity in sensorimotor regions, thought to reflect shared representation (Zaki et al., 2009). Another study used the empathic accuracy task presented both emotional and neutral video clips to the participants while their brain activity was measured with fMRI (Mackes et al., 2018). Brain activation during the perception of emotional stimuli was evident in both cognitive (bilateral superior temporal sulcus, TPJ, and temporal pole) and affective (AI, IFG) empathy-related brain regions, and activation in these areas was correlated with the stimuli's intensity. Yet empathic accuracy was found to be correlated only with activity in the cognitive empathy-related regions. This study suggests that while there is a "joint effort" of both affective and cognitive brain regions in interpreting complex naturalistic emotional social interactions, there remains a unique role of brain regions associated with cognitive empathy in the accurate interpretation of emotional states (Mackes et al., 2018).

Focusing on a very different task, that of empathy for pain (described in Section 3, Affective Empathy), researchers often use fMRI to look at shared representations, that is, brain regions that are activated when one experience pain and when one watch someone else experience pain. A network of regions that is consistently activated when experiencing pain encompasses sensory regions such as the primary and secondary somatosensory cortex (SI, SII), the anterior cingulate cortex (ACC), and anterior insula (AI). Together these are referred to as the Pain Matrix. Regions of the Pain Matrix were repeatedly found to be activated when seeing others in pain (e.g., Fallon et al., 2020; Jackson et al., 2005; Lamm et al., 2011; Singer et al., 2004, 2006; Timmers et al., 2018). This shared activation of overlapping brain regions for first-hand experience and for perceiving others' experience is believed to facilitate empathic processes. Evidence for shared activation and the association with these brain regions can also be found in research on rodents and nonhuman primates (Paradiso et al., 2021).

One criticism of the shared-representation hypothesis is that it remains unclear what these regions actually represent. For example, they may reflect more general psychological processes such as attention or arousal, which occur in both first-hand emotional experience and perception of others' emotions. Interpreting shared activation as a measure of empathy and then concluding that one shows less or more empathy in a specific task based on activation of this network is referred to as "reverse inference" (inferring psychological processes from patterns of activation). Since connecting activation patterns to actual traits or behaviors is not straightforward, one needs to be cautious with such claims; and more research is needed in order to make direct claims about the role of these shared representations (Keysers & Gazzola, 2017; Lamm et al., 2019; Zaki et al., 2016).

Electroencephalography and MEG are also used in empathy research. These methods to record electrical/magnetic activity on the scalp can represent the macroscopic activity of the surface layer of the brain underneath. Most of the brain regions described earlier are beneath the cortex and more difficult to measure with these tools. However, measuring activation over the sensorimotor cortex is possible. During rest, neurons in the sensorimotor cortex fire synchronously, resulting in oscillatory mu rhythms (rhythms in the range of 8–13 Hz). Suppression of these mu rhythms is evident in both action execution and action perception, and therefore mu suppression is thought to be a proxy of "sensorimotor simulation" or shared representation (Pineda, 2005). Despite vast evidence for mu suppression during action, its role in perception and more complex empathic processes is still under debate, with meta-analyses reaching different conclusions (Fox et al., 2016; Hobson & Bishop, 2017). Some studies have found a correlation between mu suppression and self-reported empathic concern (DiGirolamo et al., 2019) and between mu suppression and the intensity of emotional and empathy-evoking stimuli (Cheng et al., 2008; Fabi & Leuthold, 2017; Hoenen et al., 2015; Joyal et al., 2018; Moore et al., 2012; Perry et al., 2010). Mu suppression is also evident when trying to make mental-state attributions (Gutsell et al., 2020; Pineda & Hecht, 2009), and it has been shown to correlate with accurate empathic judgments (Genzer et al., 2022; Perry et al., 2017). However, the exact role of mu suppression in empathic processes remains unclear (Hobson & Bishop, 2017; Genzer et al., 2022), and replication studies with greater power are needed, together with a clearer distinction between different empathic processes.

Another common EEG technique is Event-Related Potentials (ERPs), mostly used in empathy for pain studies to discern empathy-related time-sensitive electrical brain responses. Studies commonly report modulation of the brain response in both early ERP components (such as N1, P2, N2), which are suggested to represent automatic affective-sharing processes, and late components (e.g., P3, Late Positive Potential [LPP]), believed to represent cognitive evaluation (Cui et al., 2017; Decety et al., 2010; Fabi & Leuthold, 2017; Fan & Han, 2008; Wu & Han, 2021). However, a recent meta-analysis (Coll, 2018) focused on empathy for pain ERP responses found reliable effect only for the latter (P3, LPP), not the earlier (N1, N2) components, while stressing the problem of methodological variation in quantification and statistical analysis in ERP research. In addition to findings from work on empathy for pain, LPP has long been observed to play a role in emotional processing. This neural index is believed to reflect motivational significance and subjective value of the emotional stimuli, and can be modulated by attention (Hajcak et al., 2010; Hajcak & Foti, 2020; Herbert et al., 2008).

To conclude, comparing results within social neuroscience research and especially empathy-related neural research can be rather confusing. The complexity of social processes and the different subprocesses present challenges when trying to pinpoint specific related brain activity patterns. Neural activity research suffers from various limitations, from its high cost (often resulting in small sample sizes) to overly broad definitions of empathy to differences in techniques, task demands, and cues used, which all restrict its comparability.

5 Gender Differences

Gender differences in empathy have been extensively studied, with mixed results. Several meta-analyses attempted to settle this inconsistency and support the notion that females have some advantage over males in empathy (Eisenberg & Lennon, 1983; Hall, 1978; McClure, 2000; Thompson & Voyer, 2014). However, this again depends on what definition of empathy is being used, and crucially, how empathic processes are measured. For instance, in a meta-analysis, Eisenberg and Lennon (1983) demonstrated that while large gender differences favoring females have been found in self-report questionnaires, only moderate differences were found for tasks of infant reflexive crying in response to another's distress and self-report measures in laboratory situations. Furthermore, no gender differences were observed for physiological responses or for nonverbal reactions to another's emotional state. These results could indicate that stereotypical gender roles increase our desire to appear and even see ourselves in ways "consistent" with our gender and therefore influence individuals' self-reports of empathy. For instance, men might prefer to present themselves as unemotional to others, whereas women might want to appear more empathetic, as emotional responsiveness and nurturing behavior are part of the stereotypical feminine role (Christov-Moore et al., 2014; Zhou et al., 2004).

Other studies using tasks rather than self-reports – such as focusing on emotion recognition from pictures of facial expressions – have indicated a small to moderate female superiority over males (Kirkland et al., 2013; Merten, 2005; Sasson et al., 2010). This implies that the need to see ourselves in ways consistent with our gender roles does not fully explain the female advantage in empathy. Notably, gender roles affect not only the way we desire to capture ourselves, but the way other people interact with us, which could influence the way we behave. Indeed, a recent systematic review demonstrates that gender-differentiated parenting occurs, which may lead to differences in child outcomes (Morawska, 2020).

Studies with adult participants that used more naturalistic and complex tasks, such as the empathic accuracy paradigm (see Section 2.2, Empathic Accuracy) did not find a significant difference between females and males (Graham & Ickes, 1997; Grant et al., 2018; Jospe et al., 2020). Interestingly, a female advantage in empathic accuracy was found in studies in which perceivers were asked to rate how well they thought they had inferred the target's mental state. This minor difference in the instructions could increase females' awareness of being evaluated on their empathic ability, and by that, increase their motivation to perform well in alignment with their gender roles (Graham & Ickes, 1997; Klein & Hodges, 2001). This explanation is reinforced by Thomas and Maio's (2008) findings that females were more accurate in inferring the other's emotional states only after being given information that challenged their empathic skills as women.

Importantly, growing research acknowledges that gender is not always a binary structure, and that people could have gender identities that differ from their birth-assigned gender (e.g., transgender, gender fluid, or nonbinary; Chew et al., 2020; Diamond, 2020). Nevertheless, research on nonbinary gender and empathy is scarce, shows mixed results (Spies et al., 2016), and is often underpowered. Future studies could benefit from looking at gender and sex independently and/or looking at gender as a continuum and examining its effects on the different facets of empathy (Ho & Mussap, 2019).

To conclude, there is some evidence that females are more empathic than males, but the degree of this advantage varies significantly and is most evident in self-report measures. One explanation for these discrepancies is that females are indeed better than males at understanding others' emotions in real life, but this advantage is rather small and requires large sample sizes, or a clear motivational factor, to be revealed. The underline cause for the females' advantage is under debate, and it is still unclear whether this advantage is caused by congenital factors, social factors, or a combination of both.

6 Biases and Limitations of Empathy

While empathy has many advantages in our everyday lives, from understanding our spouse, child, or colleague, it is also prone to many biases. As cognitive and social psychologists have long noted, unlike a computer or video recorder we do not perceive the world as it is but rather pay attention to things that are most important to us, interpret the world based on our prior beliefs and knowledge, and prioritize those who are closer to us. For example, think of the scenario described in the beginning of the Element. If this were a video you were watching, and you perceived the crying woman to be around your age, with your gender and ethnicity, or maybe she wore similar clothes to your own, your empathy toward her would probably be increased compared to perceiving her as being very different from you (see also Section 3.3, Context Matters). Since our empathy is likely to affect our decisions and prosocial behavior, acknowledging these biases and trying to avoid them is of paramount importance. It is because of these biases that the renowned psychologist Paul Bloom gave his book the provocative name *Against Empathy* (Bloom, 2017), warning people, and especially policy makers, to be careful when making decisions based on their affective empathic responses (see also Decety, 2021).

One of the most consistent findings in the literature is that people's judgments of others' mental states are anchored on their own state, a phenomenon termed *egocentric bias* (Epley & Eyal, 2019). Whereas considering one's own perspective is an automatic, almost effortless process, taking the perspective of another requires cognitive resources and effort (Epley et al., 2004). When trying to understand the other's perspective, one often tries to imagine what s/he would feel in the same situation. When the two perspectives are incongruent – for example, when one finds a situation amusing while the other finds it horrifying or offensive – it is more difficult to accurately identify the other's perspective (Epley et al., 2004), and members of a pair would most likely judge the other's emotional state as more similar to their own (Clark et al., 2017; Trilla et al., 2021).

Another consistent finding is the effect of *intergroup empathy bias*, that is, people's tendency to distinguish others as in- versus out-group members and to modulate their own empathy levels in favor of the in-group (Fourie et al., 2017). This bias has been found when one perceives others as belonging to a socially distant group, such as a different racial or national group (Cikara et al., 2011), or even to a rival sports fan group (Hein et al., 2010). The bias is reflected not only in behavior but also in various physiological indices, offering unique insights into when and why people empathize less with out-group members (Vollberg & Cikara, 2018). For example, both fMRI and EEG studies have revealed that neural signatures that are thought to be related to experience sharing show stronger responses when study participants watch pictures of in-group members versus out-group members experiencing pain (for reviews, see Han, 2018; Volberg & Cikara, 2018). These results were replicated across cultures (including Chinese [Sheng et al., 2014], Australian [Contreras-Huerta et al., 2013], European [Azevedo et al., 2013], and Middle Eastern populations [Levy et al., 2016]) and social groups (such as sports fans; Hein et al., 2010). Other studies have shown that social class may affect empathic accuracy. In a line of studies, Kraus and colleagues (2010) show that individuals of a lower social class are more empathically accurate in judging the emotions of other people. The association between social class and empathic accuracy was explained by the tendency for lower-class individuals to explain social events in terms of features of the external environment, and thus focus on these external factors more (see also Stellar et al., 2012).

To conclude, empathy is not impartial in the sense that it does not passively convey the world to us. Like other forms of perception and cognition, it is constrained by our physiological states, biased by evolutionary processes, and affected by our past experiences and current values and motivations. Importantly, acknowledging the limitations of the empathic processes can help in trying to reduce their effects or find interventions to help overcome them. Applying different social psychology–based intervention (Weisz & Zaki, 2017), for example, changing belief about empathy as being limited in inter-group contexts (Hasson et al., 2022), can help reduce bias and enhance our empathy toward different others. Additionally, we can try to develop these skills and enhance our general capacity for understanding others by asking for feedback (Eyal et al., 2018; Israelashvili & Perry, 2021), being aware of our biases, having a motivation to change (Weisz & Zaki, 2018), and even engaging in arts (Amir, 2022).

7 Clinical Conditions

Findings from clinical conditions are highly valued in the effort to understand the multifaceted concept of empathy on the one hand and to clearly differentiate between clinical profiles on the other. Deficits in empathic abilities are prevalent across many clinical conditions and in some cases can stem from differences in perceiving the social world. Some clinical conditions are temporary. If one is feeling more depressed or anxious, this may elevate their personal distress and obscure their ability to capture or relate to positive emotions of others (Guhn et al., 2020). In contrast, people who suffer from social anxiety are often sensitive to very subtle cues in the other and show heightened affective empathy, but their interpretation may be exaggerated and result in inaccurate judgment of the other's emotional state (for a review, see Pittelkow et al., 2021). Other clinical conditions such as autism, psychopathy or schizophrenia are more permanent and stable throughout life, and they are associated by definition with pronounced dysfunction in social perception (Baron-Cohen, 2010; Bird & Viding, 2014; Blair, 2005, 2010; Brüne, 2005; Horan & Green, 2019; Tandon et al., 2013).

Schizophrenia is characterized by a marked and stable deficit in many aspects of social perception, including emotion recognition and empathic abilities (Achim et al., 2011; Brüne, 2005; Derntl et al., 2009; Green et al., 2005, 2012; Kohler et al., 2010). These social-perception deficits are apparent in the prodrome to psychosis (Amminger, Schäfer, Papageorgiou et al., 2012; Amminger, Schäfer, Klier et al., 2012; Thompson et al., 2011, 2012) and seriously impede social competence (Brüne et al., 2007; Smith et al., 2012). Some suggest that both cognitive and affective aspects of empathy are impaired in schizophrenia (Bonfils et al., 2017; Derntl et al., 2009), whereas others claim that schizophrenia and psychopathy are characterized by deficits in affective empathy alone (Blair, 2005; Jones et al., 2010; Shamay-Tsoory et al., 2007; see Bonfils et al., 2016, for a meta-analysis).

In autism, a neurodevelopmental disorder characterized by social and communication impairments, most researchers suggest that the more pronounced deficits are cognitive ones, that is, deficits in accurately understanding the emotional states of others (Baron-Cohen et al., 2001.; Dziobek et al., 2008; Fridenson-Hayo et al., 2016; Gleichgerrcht et al., 2013; Uljarevic & Hamilton, 2013), with affective empathy being relatively spared (Dziobek et al., 2008; Rueda et al., 2015; but see Adler et al., 2015; Grove et al., 2014). Indeed, even high-functioning autistic adults who can pass simplified lab tests, often exhibit clear deficits in naturalistic empathic accuracy tasks (Adler et al., 2015; Demurie et al., 2011; Ponnet et al., 2004, 2005, 2008; Roeyers et al., 2001). Importantly, researchers and clinicians are now thinking of autistic traits as being on a spectrum, with a disorder on one end and varying levels of autistic traits on the continuum (Pellicano & de Houting, 2022; Whitehouse et al., 2011). Therefore, neurotypical individuals, people with typical development, could also have different levels of autistic traits. Indeed, even in neurotypicals, autistic traits are associated with poorer empathic-accuracy abilities (aan het Rot & Hogenelst, 2014; Bartz et al., 2010, 2019).

Milton, a sociologist studying empathy and autism, coined the term "the double Empathy Problem", referring to the idea that empathy is a two-way street. Just as people with autism may have difficulties in perceiving the emotional states of neurotypicals, neurotypicals may find it difficult to understand autistic people or other people who are different from them (Milton, 2012). In fact, as previously mentioned, our perception of others' emotional states is often biased by different factors, including our group affiliation or how similar the other person is to us. With most research to date focused on how good or bad autistics are at understanding neurotypical others, recent work attempts to also study how well neurotypicals understand autistics (and how well autistics understand each other).

8 Future Directions; Where the Field Is Going

The future of empathy research will likely involve a deeper exploration of the theoretical and conceptual questions at the heart of the field. One such question concerns the nature of empathy itself, and whether it represents several discrete cognitive and affective processes, or a combination of intertwined processes. Another question may be how it affects and is affected by additional senses, beyond vision and audition, and what factors contribute to individual differences in empathy. Additionally, there may be more focus on exploring the cultural and contextual factors that shape empathy, as well as the ethical implications of empathy research and its applications, especially as technology catches up with human abilities. As researchers continue to tackle these and other questions, they may develop more nuanced and complex models of empathy that can better account for its function outside of the laboratory and its role in social behavior and relationships. Ultimately, the future of empathy research holds the promise of deepening our understanding of what it means to be human, and of promoting greater empathy and compassion in our interactions with others. In this last section, we briefly describe current trends in the field as we see them evolving, as well as some of our own general takes on the future of empathy research.

8.1 Other Senses

The world is becoming increasingly reliant on video communication, particularly in light of recent global events that have accelerated this trend. However, it is important to recognize that video communication is limited in its ability to convey important sensory information, such as touch and smell. Understanding the role of these sensory experiences in our social lives is an important area of future research that can inform the development of more effective and holistic forms of communication. Smell and social chemo-signals are rarely used to study empathy. Nevertheless, there is evidence of the effect of chemo-signals on our ability to share others' states. The emotional state of others can be perceived from chemo-signals and shared by the sniffer. Smelling fear or anxiety-related odorants in another can lead to greater anxiety in the perceiver (Prehn-Kristensen et al., 2009; Quintana et al., 2019; Rocha et al., 2018). Smelling sweat from a person who went through a stressful event can exert an enhanced empathic response compared to sport-related sweat (Hoenen et al., 2018). On the other hand, positive emotional chemo-signals, such as sweat produced while observing positive videos, elicited happier facial expressions by the sniffer (de Groot et al., 2015). The field of socio-chemistry – studying nonverbal social communication by odorants – is rapidly growing and recently has increased its contribution to our understanding of empathic processes (de Groot et al., 2020; Hofer et al., 2020) and social processes in humans in general (Gelstein et al., 2011; Mishor et al., 2021; Ravreby et al., 2022). As the social world is increasingly intertwined with technology, and people work, learn, and socialize remotely via online platforms, examining what aspects of the empathic processes are mediated by the different senses becomes a timely question.

8.2 Individual and Cultural Differences

Research in empathy, as in other fields, started with examining the average effects or the extremes (such as clinical manifestations). However, once a research field is more mature, individual differences that affect how we perceive people around us and react to them become interesting as well. For example, studies focusing on empathy for pain produce evidence for the connection between individual differences in perceivers' first-hand pain sensitivity and the ability to share others' pain (see Section 3.2, Empathy for Pain). Recent findings show that having a sibling with disabilities, whether social or other, enhances empathic abilities and prosocial behavior (Orm et al., 2022; Perenc & Peczkowski, 2018) and perhaps specifically better understanding of others (i.e., cognitive empathy; Rum et al., 2022). Such studies confirm that how we perceive the (social) world around us is highly dependent on our own experience and history. They also suggest that empathy is a flexible process that can be learned and improved, especially when sharing your childhood with someone who is different. This could have important implications in fields such as education and organizational behavior.

Other lines of research focus on individual differences in eye-gaze when trying to decipher the emotions of others. For example, Yitzhak and colleagues (2020) reported consistent evidence from four groups of observers that differed in their distribution of fixations on face regions. In line with previous studies, they found that different facial emotion categories evoked distinct distributions of fixations according to their diagnostic facial regions (e.g., anger is more pronounced in the eyes). However, individual distinctive patterns of fixations were not correlated with emotion recognition: Individuals who strongly focused on the eyes or the mouth achieved comparable emotion recognition accuracy. Other studies expanded this work to look at processing of cues that were completely outside the face and found similar consistent effects: While some people focused mainly on the face to understand the other's emotions, others consistently looked more at body posture or other contextual cues (Lecker & Aviezer, 2021; Lecker et al., 2020).

Finally, it is important to remember that most research in psychology is still done in Western Educated Industrial Rich and Democratic (WEIRD) populations (Henrich et al., 2010). In recent years, there is a growing understanding of the importance of studying diverse populations, which indeed may perceive the world in a different manner. A number of studies focusing on cultural variation in cognitive processes suggest that, as a whole, different cultures foster quite different modes of cognitive processing (Kitayama et al., 2003; Markus & Kitayama, 1991; Nisbett et al., 2001). Several recent studies show the effect of cultural differences on empathic capacities and empathic reactions (Atkins et al., 2016; Chan & Cassels, 2010) and the interaction of culture with other factors such as gender (Zhao et al., 2021), stressing the importance of including and further examine cultural variations in empathy research (for a recent review see Jami et al., 2023). Studying other cultures will enable us to define which aspects of the empathic process are universal, how much is culture-specific, and how flexible these processes are.

8.3 Computational Tools

Psychology research as a field is moving toward integrating computational tools-based methods to create, assess, and predict behaviors and psychological processes. These computational tools often require mathematical and statistical understanding as well as programming knowledge. The next section presents a general description of two main approaches for computational tools: mathematical modeling and machine learning. As each of these methods is drawn from a different scientific field, their goals and solutions to achieve these goals are somewhat different. We address some of these differences and emphasize the value of these tools for promoting research in psychology in general and social cognition in particular.

Mathematical modeling is a term borrowed from theoretical physics. Researchers in this field attempt to describe or predict natural phenomena using a set of equations defining the various forces affecting the system and the relationships between these forces (Carnap, 1995). Each variable in these equations represents a component in the hypothesized processes (Sherman et al., 2021). We can simulate expected behavior based on these equations, then examine how similar the simulation results are to behavioral data collected in the lab or field. This approach allows us to parametrically evaluate our theoretical model.

While mathematical modeling is a valuable tool, the need for highly advanced mathematical knowledge makes it less common in psychological research. Some work has been conducted using mathematical modeling in a more broad social context. We will briefly describe some of these studies to demonstrate the beneficial contribution of mathematical modeling in psychological research and hope that future research will use this tool to investigate empathy as well.

Noy and colleagues (2011) used mathematical modeling to investigate the mechanisms that underlie synchronized joint improvisation, that is, the creation of novel joint action or movement between two individuals even without a designated leader. From a behavioral perspective, results indicated that expert improvisers achieve better precision and performance when there is no designated leader than when a leader is designated. The authors provided a mathematical solution based on control theory that enables these results and suggested that the mechanism is based on mutual agreement on future motion in mirrored reactive–predictive controllers.

The requirement for a strong and clear theoretical basis when using mathematical modeling can encourage researchers to generate theories for complex problems; mathematical modeling then provides tools that numerically evaluate the theories. Moreover, it can facilitate comparison of different theories and assessing which theory best explains the observed data. An example of such an algorithm is based on the theoretical model of predictive coding. This model applies a theoretical framework from sensory perception to different neuronal and psychological processes (Kliemann & Adolphs, 2018). Predictive coding suggests that the way we perceive the world is based not on sensory input alone but also is influenced by predictions generated by internal models. The actual sensory input is compared to the predicted sensory data, resulting in discrepancy or "error" that in turn is used to update the internal model. The model adaptation is an iterative process, and the model optimizes as error minimizes and therefore produces better predictions for the sensory input (Shipp, 2016). This model could be adapted to the social world in an effort to explain how we infer others' emotions and intentions (Ishida et al., 2015; Kilner et al., 2007; Kliemann & Adolphs, 2018; Shipp, 2016).

Mathematical modeling could also be used to evaluate different theoretical explanations for a phenomenon in the world. For instance, Vishne and colleagues (2021) used mathematical modeling to evaluate two opposite theoretical explanations based on a Bayesian framework for the social, motor and perceptual deficits of autistic individuals. The first theory implies that these difficulties reflect oversensitivity to prediction errors, and the second theory suggests that the underlying reason for these difficulties is the slow updating of such errors. To examine these two theories, Vishne and colleagues used a paced finger-tapping task, a synchronization task that requires the use of recent sensory information for rapid error correction. Computational modeling tools allowed the researchers to disentangle the contributions of error correction from that of noise in keeping temporal intervals and executing motor responses. Trial-by-trial modeling revealed typical noise levels in interval representations and motor responses. However, the rate of error correction was reduced, impeding autistic individuals' synchronization ability. Therefore, these results provide support for the slow updating of internal representations in autism.

The concept of machine learning is taken from computer science and refers to a set of techniques that improve system performance by learning from experience (i.e., data) via computational methods. The main task of machine learning is to develop a learning algorithm that builds models from data that can make predictions on new observations (Zhou, 2021). Note that some machine learning techniques also incorporate mathematical modeling and strong theoretical basis (Chaudhary et al., 2021). However, other machine learning techniques, such as deep learning techniques do not necessarily require preselected features and can automatically extract the significant features from raw input for a problem at hand (Indolia et al., 2018). Although this could be considered a significant advantage when one wants to predict an outcome, it also means that it could be difficult to deduce the mechanism and theoretical model that underlies the result or the process that was investigated, as deep learning algorithms often create layers of "black box" (Shwartz-Ziv & Tishby, 2017). Nevertheless, this approach allows us to examine general theoretical models, even if some details of the model remain unclear to the researcher at the end of the algorithm's learning process.

Together with recent technological advances which have facilitated easier collection and sharing of large-scale audio, visual, and text data, concurrent advances in signal processing and machine learning techniques enable analyzing complex human behaviors such as empathic behavior from diverse multimodal data (Xiao et al., 2016). These machine learning techniques frequently use a data-driven approach to automatically map measured behavioral cues to empathy ratings. The models' predictions are then typically compared to human expert ratings on new or held-out interactions not seen in model construction (Duda et al., 2012). Research on empathic processes, specifically related to cognitive empathy, could benefit from deep learning techniques that are already used for image recognition, speech recognition, sentiment analysis, natural language understanding, signal processing, and face recognition (Indolia et al., 2018; Xiao et al., 2016). For example, Chakravarthula and colleagues (2015) have found that a dynamic model that considers the therapist's likelihood to transition between high vs. low- behavioral empathy states (perceived as strongly empathic vs. or nonempathic) over the therapeutic session time results in improved predictions compared to a static model that assumes a fixed degree of empathy throughout an interaction. Importantly, machine learning can also be used to validate the behavioral results of an experimental procedure or add additional information to it. For instance, Drimalla and colleagues (2019) behaviorally found that facial expressions mimicry, measured by facial electromyography while viewing photographs depicting individuals in emotionally charged situations, was stronger for an affective empathy condition ("to what degree do you empathize with the individual in the photo") compared to a cognitive empathy condition ("try to infer the mental state of the person in the picture"). Moreover, the correlation patterns between mimicry intensity to empathy scores were different for each condition: Affective empathy was correlated to mimicry intensity only for positive valence stimuli, while cognitive empathy was correlated to mimicry intensity for both positive and negative valence stimuli. Accordingly, the model predicted the condition in which a facial expression had been presented from the muscle activity with an accuracy of 70 percent, reinforcing the experimental behavioral results for differences in mimicry manifestation in cognitive and affective empathy.

Using computations to model psychological processes could provide a powerful tool for shedding light on the relationship and causal links between concepts, such as cognitive and affective empathy, or empathy and prosocial behavior. These formulations may help form new predictions about the processes being studied. Moreover, computational models of empathy are being used today by researchers of artificial intelligence (AI) who are trying to create empathic computers or robots – that is, computers with the ability to infer human emotions accurately.

8.4 Human–AI Interactions

The combination of AI and empathy research has the potential to revolutionize how we understand and approach human emotions and social interactions. Empathic robots may have immense value in fields like telemedicine or other remote care (Dahl & Boulos, 2013; Eysenbach, 2023). Moreover, with the power of AI, we can analyze vast amounts of data and gain new insights into the neural and cognitive processes involved in empathy. Machine learning algorithms can be trained to recognize patterns in complex emotional data, allowing us to better understand the factors that shape empathy and how it develops over time. Additionally, AI can be used to develop more sophisticated and personalized interventions for individuals with empathy deficits, such as virtual reality experiences that simulate social interactions and provide opportunities for practice and feedback. By leveraging the strengths of AI and empathy research, we can deepen our understanding of human emotions and behavior, and develop innovative solutions that promote greater empathy and compassion in our interactions with others.

A few years ago, cognitive science students were taught that a computer's visual perception and discrimination abilities are far from that of humans, but today we know that computers can easily discriminate objects, understand language, play chess, and even create original works of art and literature (Cetinic et al., 2022; Nath et al., 2022). It is not a question of if but when computers will be able to perceive our emotions relatively accurately, or at least as accurately as humans. While going into the different algorithms is beyond the scope of this section, it is worth noting that there are encouraging results trying to accurately infer emotions from language (Ong et al., 2019), vocal sounds (Brooks et al., 2023), facial expressions (Shvimmer, 2022), or a combination of these (Ong et al., 2019). To build AI tools that understand human emotions, researchers must overcome the challenge of modeling emotion dynamics. Ong et al. (2019) offer a comprehensive review of contemporary timeseries modeling approaches that are used or can be used productively in affective computing. The frequent use of video cameras on smartphones and computers will enable emotion monitoring in real time, and any use of additional sensors (such as galvanic skin response or heart rate) will increase accuracy (for a review, see Tzafilkou et al., 2021).

A different aspect of empathic AI relates to computers expressing empathy (regardless of whether the AI accurately perceived one's emotions). With the advancement of tools that convincedly mimic human faces, speech and facial expressions (e.g., D-ID, a digital people platform; www.d-id.com/), and human conversation (artificial chatbots such as chatGPT), computers will soon be able to at least exhibit empathy quite convincingly, and could be used for additional social support when human support is missing or impossible (Xygkou et al., 2023).

As AI and empathy research continue to progress, there are several ethical questions that must be considered in the development and implementation of empathic AI. One concern is the potential for empathic AI to be used for nefarious purposes, such as manipulating or exploiting individuals' emotions for financial or political gain. Additionally, there may be concerns about privacy and data security, as empathic AI relies heavily on collecting and analyzing personal data (Ong, 2021). There are also questions about the potential impact of empathic AI on human–human interactions, and whether it may lead to a devaluation of human empathy and emotional intelligence. Finally, there may be questions about the responsibility of empathic AI, and who should be held accountable for any negative consequences that arise from its use (Bryson, 2019). As we continue to develop and integrate empathic AI into our society, it is essential that we carefully consider and address these ethical questions to ensure that we create a future that is both technologically advanced and ethically responsible.

8.5 General Comments and Our Own Take on the Field

The last decade has brought an ongoing shift from highly controlled stimuli (e.g., still pictures of posed facial expressions) to more natural ones (Schilbach et al., 2013; Wheatley et al., 2019; Zaki & Ochsner, 2012). We believe this shift is particularly important in complex dyadic social behavior, such as in experiencing empathy. We thus expect to see more research focused on empathy within dyadic and group dynamics in more naturalistic settings. This goes hand in hand with advances in technologies that enable mobile-based daily sampling (e.g., Depow et al., 2021), mobile eye-tracking (Pérez-Edgar et al., 2020), and mobile fNIRS systems (Pinti et al., 2020), which allows researchers to collect self-report and physiological measurements in real-world social interactions. The growing use of virtual reality (VR) in the lab will also facilitate measuring empathy and related constructs in naturalistic yet controlled environments and ultimately may be able to actually enable one to more realistically "walk in the other's shoes" (induced perspective-taking; Cohen et al., 2021; Fusaro et al., 2016; Herrera et al., 2018; Young et al., 2021). Finally, advances in statistical modeling, such as the social-relations modeling (SRM; Koster et al., 2019) that accounts for the variance of each partner as well as the unique dyad, will help us better explain the data obtained from these complex multiparticipant designs.

Note, though, that there is always a tradeoff between well-controlled, repeated-measures studies in the lab and a more naturalistic research design. To give just one example, when using two- to three-minute-long emotional videos, only a small number of videos can be viewed until the experiment is too long and the participant loses attention. Which exact stimuli to use becomes crucial, and so does the question of how much the experimenter can generalize or infer from the results to other conditions. This is less of a problem when it's possible to use an average of 100 still pictures of diverse faces, and so forth, but then you lose the complexity of an unfolding emotional story. This problem can be partially addressed with open science and sharing of data. Future research will no doubt make use of techniques with higher resolution, such as 7-Tesla fMRI (Viessmann & Polimeni, 2021), electrocorticography (ECoG; Perry et al., 2017), and single cell recordings (Jamali et al., 2021; Mukamel et al., 2010). But more importantly, studies would benefit from collaborations allowing larger sample sizes, along with a combination of neural and behavioral measures to better corroborate the functional meaning of different brain activation patterns (Zaki & Ochsner, 2012). By combining data from different labs, it will become easier to analyze a wide collection of naturalistic data, even if collected independently, and to determine which results are robust and hold across labs, cultures, and contexts.

9 Conclusion

Empathy is an integral part of humans' daily lives. We perceive the emotional states of the people around us (our spouse, family members, colleagues, friends), and we express our own feelings to them. More than understanding others, we often "feel with" them. Our perception of others' emotions influences our reactions, fostering prosocial behavior, but it can also draw from a variety of biases: We empathize with those close to or similar to us, and our empathy is influenced by our physiological state. As research evolves, controlled studies will likely be combined with more naturalistic ones, utilizing technologies such as virtual reality and using machine learning and mathematical models to predict behavior. Collaborations and meta-analyses should be embraced in neuroimaging research, along with designs that closely link brain activity with behavior. The better we understand empathic processes and their underlying mechanisms, the more effective the interventions that can be developed, both for clinical populations and the general public.

References

aan het Rot, M., & Hogenelst, K. (2014). The influence of affective empathy and autism spectrum traits on empathic accuracy. *PLoS ONE, 9*(6), 1–7. https://doi.org/10.1371/JOURNAL.PONE.0098436.

Abramson, L., Uzefovsky, F., Toccaceli, V., & Knafo-Noam, A. (2020). The genetic and environmental origins of emotional and cognitive empathy: Review and meta-analyses of twin studies. *Neuroscience & Biobehavioral Reviews, 114*, 113–133. https://doi.org/10.1016/J.NEUBIOREV.2020.03.023.

Achim, A. M., Ouellet, R., Roy, M. A., & Jackson, P. L. (2011). Assessment of empathy in first-episode psychosis and meta-analytic comparison with previous studies in schizophrenia. *Psychiatry Research, 190*(1), 3–8. https://doi.org/10.1016/J.PSYCHRES.2010.10.030.

Adler, N., Dvash, J., & Shamay-Tsoory, S. G. (2015). Empathic embarrassment accuracy in autism spectrum disorder. *Autism Research, 8*(3), 241–249. https://doi.org/10.1002/AUR.1439.

Aguado, L., Fernández-Cahill, M., Román, F. J., Blanco, I., & de Echegaray, J. (2018). Evaluative and psychophysiological responses to short film clips of different emotional content. *Journal of Psychophysiology, 32*(1), 1–19. https://doi.org/10.1027/0269-8803/A000180.

Akitsuki, Y., & Decety, J. (2009). Social context and perceived agency affects empathy for pain: An event-related fMRI investigation. *NeuroImage, 47*(2), 722–734. https://doi.org/10.1016/J.NEUROIMAGE.2009.04.091.

Allison, P. D., & Liker, J. K. (1982). Analyzing sequential categorical data on dyadic interaction: A comment on Gottman. *Psychological Bulletin, 91*, 393–403.

Amir, E. (2022). Raising empathy: Synthesizing performance art and social psychology. *AMASS Conference: Dialogical Arts through Sustainable Communities, 7*(1). https://doi.org/10.2/JQUERY.MIN.JS.

Amminger, G. P., Schäfer, M. R., Klier, C. M., et al. (2012). Facial and vocal affect perception in people at ultra-high risk of psychosis, first-episode schizophrenia and healthy controls. *Early Intervention in Psychiatry, 6*(4), 450–454. https://doi.org/10.1111/J.1751-7893.2012.00362.X.

Amminger, G. P., Schäfer, M. R., Papageorgiou, K., et al. (2012). Emotion recognition in individuals at clinical high-risk for schizophrenia. *Schizophrenia Bulletin, 38*(5), 1030–1039. https://doi.org/10.1093/SCHBUL/SBR015.

Anders, S., Heinzle, J., Weiskopf, N., Ethofer, T., & Haynes, J. D. (2011). Flow of affective information between communicating brains. *NeuroImage, 54*(1), 439–446. https://doi.org/10.1016/J.NEUROIMAGE.2010.07.004.

Atias, D., Todorov, A., Liraz, S., et al. (2019). Loud and unclear: Intense real-life vocalizations during affective situations are perceptually ambiguous and contextually malleable. *Journal of Experimental Psychology: General, 148*(10), 1842–1848. https://doi.org/10.1037/xge0000535.

Atkins, D., Uskul, A. K., & Cooper, N. R. (2016). Culture shapes empathic responses to physical and social pain. *Emotion, 16*(5), 587–601.

Atkinson, A. P., Dittrich, W. H., Gemmell, A. J., & Young, A. W. (2004). Emotion perception from dynamic and static body expressions in point-light and full-light displays. *Perception, 33*(6), 717–746. https://doi .org/10.1068/P5096.

Avenanti, A., Bueti, D., Galati, G., & Aglioti, S. M. (2005). Transcranial magnetic stimulation highlights the sensorimotor side of empathy for pain. *Nature Neuroscience, 8*(7), 955–960. https://doi.org/10.1038/nn1481.

Avenanti, A., Paluello, I. M., Bufalari, I., & Aglioti, S. M. (2006). Stimulus-driven modulation of motor-evoked potentials during observation of others' pain. *NeuroImage, 32*(1), 316–324. https://doi.org/10.1016/j.neuroimage .2006.03.010.

Aviezer, H., Ensenberg, N., & Hassin, R. R. (2017). The inherently contextual-ized nature of facial emotion perception. *Current Opinion in Psychology, 17*, 47–54. https://doi.org/10.1016/J.COPSYC.2017.06.006.

Aviezer, H., Hassin, R. R., Ryan, J., et al. (2008). Angry, disgusted, or afraid? *Psychological Science, 19*(7), 724–732. https://doi.org/10.1111/J.1467-9280 .2008.02148.X.

Azevedo, R. T., Macaluso, E., Avenanti, A., et al. (2013). Their pain is not our pain: Brain and autonomic correlates of empathic resonance with the pain of same and different race individuals. *Human Brain Mapping, 34*(12), 3168–3181. https://doi.org/10.1002/HBM.22133.

Banks, S. J., Bellerose, J., Douglas, D., & Jones-Gotman, M. (2012). Bilateral skin conductance responses to emotional faces. *Applied Psychophysiology Biofeedback, 37*(3), 145–152. https://doi.org/10.1007/S10484-011-9177-7.

Banse, R., & Scherer, K. R. (1996). Acoustic profiles in vocal emotion expression. *Journal of Personality and Social Psychology, 70*(3), 614–636. https://doi.org/10.1037/0022-3514.70.3.614.

Baron-Cohen, S. (2010). Empathizing, systemizing, and the extreme male brain theory of autism. *Progress in Brain Research, 186*, 167–175. https://doi.org/ 10.1016/B978-0-444-53630-3.00011-7.

Baron-Cohen, S., & Wheelwright, S. (2004). The empathy quotient: An inves-tigation of adults with Asperger syndrome or high functioning autism, and normal sex differences. *Journal of Autism and Developmental Disorders, 34*(2), 163–175.

Baron-Cohen, S., Wheelwright, S., Hill, J., Raste, Y., & Plumb, I. (2001). The "reading the mind in the eyes" test revised version: A study with normal adults, and adults with Asperger syndrome or high-functioning autism. *The Journal of Child Psychology and Psychiatry and Allied Disciplines*, 42(2), 241–251. https://doi.org/10.1017/S0021963001006643.

Barrett, L. F., Mesquita, B., & Gendron, M. (2011). Context in emotion perception. *Current Directions in Psychological Science*, 20(5), 286–290. https://doi.org/10.1177/0963721411422522.

Barone, D. F., Hutchings, P. S., Kimmel, H. J., et al. (2005). Increasing empathic accuracy through practice and feedback in a clinical interviewing course. *Journal of Social and Clinical Psychology*, 24(2), 156–171.

Bartz, J. A., Nitschke, J. P., Krol, S. A., & Tellier, P. P. (2019). Oxytocin selectively improves empathic accuracy: A replication in men and novel insights in women. *Biological Psychiatry: Cognitive Neuroscience and Neuroimaging*, 4(12), 1042–1048. https://doi.org/10.1016/J.BPSC.2019.01.014.

Bartz, J. A., Zaki, J., Bolger, N., et al. (2010). Oxytocin selectively improves empathic accuracy. *Psychological Science*, 21(10), 1426–1428. https://doi.org/10.1177/0956797610383439.

Bastiaansen, J. A. C. J., Thioux, M., & Keysers, C. (2009). Evidence for mirror systems in emotions. *Philosophical Transactions of the Royal Society B: Biological Sciences*, 364(1528), 2391–2404. https://doi.org/10.1098/rstb.2009.0058.

Bastian, B., Jetten, J., & Ferris, L. J. (2014). Pain as social glue: Shared pain increases cooperation. *Psychological Science*, 25(11), 2079–2085. https://doi.org/10.1177/09567976211004119.

Batson, C. D. (1991). *The Altruism Question: Toward a Social-Psychological Answer*. Psychology Press.

Batson, C. D., Lishner, D. A., & Stocks, E. L. (2015). The empathy–altruism hypothesis. In D. A. Schroeder & Graziano, W. G (Eds.), *The Oxford Handbook of Prosocial Behavior*. Oxford University Press, pp. 259–281. https://doi.org/10.1093/oxfordhb/9780195399813.013.023.

Ben-Simon, E., & Walker, M. P. (2018). Sleep loss causes social withdrawal and loneliness. *Nature Communications*, 9(1), 1–9. https://doi.org/10.1038/s41467-018-05377-0.

Bernat, E., Patrick, C. J., Benning, S. D., & Tellegen, A. (2006). Effects of picture content and intensity on affective physiological response. *Psychophysiology*, 43(1), 93–103. https://doi.org/10.1111/J.1469-8986.2006.00380.X.

Bird, G., & Viding, E. (2014). The self to other model of empathy: Providing a new framework for understanding empathy impairments in psychopathy, autism, and alexithymia. *Neuroscience and Biobehavioral Reviews*, *47*, 520–532. https://doi.org/10.1016/j.neubiorev.2014.09.021.

Blair, R. J. R. (2005). Responding to the emotions of others: Dissociating forms of empathy through the study of typical and psychiatric populations. *Consciousness and Cognition*, *14*(4), 698–718. https://doi.org/10.1016/J .CONCOG.2005.06.004.

Blair, R. J. R. (2010). Neuroimaging of psychopathy and antisocial behavior: A targeted review. *Current Psychiatry Reports*, *12*(1), 76–82. https://doi.org/ 10.1007/S11920-009-0086-X.

Blakemore, S. J., Bristow, D., Bird, G., Frith, C., & Ward, J. (2005). Somatosensory activations during the observation of touch and a case of vision-touch synaesthesia. *Brain*, *128*(7), 1571–1583. https://doi.org/ 10.1093/brain/awh500.

Bloom, P. (2017). *Against Empathy: The Case for Rational Compassion*. Random House.

Blunden, H., & Brodsky, A. (2021). Beyond the emoticon: Are there unintentional cues of emotion in email? *Personality and Social Psychology Bulletin*, *47*(4), 565–579. https://doi.org/10.1177/0146167220936054.

Bonfils, K. A., Lysaker, P. H., Minor, K. S., & Salyers, M. P. (2016). Affective empathy in schizophrenia: A meta-analysis. *Schizophrenia Research*, *175*(1–3), 109–117. https://doi.org/10.1016/J.SCHRES.2016.03.037.

Bonfils, K. A., Lysaker, P. H., Minor, K. S., & Salyers, M. P. (2017). Empathy in schizophrenia: A meta-analysis of the Interpersonal Reactivity Index. *Psychiatry Research*, *249*, 293–303. https://doi.org/10.1016/J.PSYCHRES .2016.12.033.

Bradley, M. M., & Lang, P. J. (1994). Measuring emotion: The self-assessment manikin and the semantic differential. *Journal of Behavior Therapy and Experimental Psychiatry*, *25*(1), 49–59.

Britton, J. C., Taylor, S. F., Berridge, K. C., Mikels, J. A., & Liberzon, I. (2006). Differential subjective and psychophysiological responses to socially and nonsocially generated emotional stimuli. *Emotion*, *6*(1), 150–155. https://doi .org/10.1037/1528-3542.6.1.150.

Brooks, J. A., Tzirakis, P., Baird, A., et al. (2023). Deep learning reveals what vocal bursts express in different cultures. *Nature Human Behaviour*, *7*(2), 240–250.

Brouwer, A. M., Van Wouwe, N., Mühl, C., van Erp, J., & Toet, A. (2013). Perceiving blocks of emotional pictures and sounds: effects on physiological variables. *Frontiers in Human Neuroscience*, *7*, 1–10.

Brüne, M. (2005). "Theory of mind" in schizophrenia: A review of the literature. *Schizophrenia Bulletin*, *31*(1), 21–42. https://doi.org/10.1093/SCHBUL/SBI002.

Brüne, M., Abdel-Hamid, M., Lehmkämper, C., & Sonntag, C. (2007). Mental state attribution, neurocognitive functioning, and psychopathology: What predicts poor social competence in schizophrenia best? *Schizophrenia Research, 92*(1–3), 151–159. https://doi.org/10.1016/J.SCHRES.2007.01.006.

Bryson, J. J. (2019). The past decade and future of AI's impact on society. *Towards a New Enlightenment, 11*, 150–185.

Byom, L. J., & Mutlu, B. (2013). Theory of mind: Mechanisms, methods, and new directions. *Frontiers in Human Neuroscience, 7*, 1–12. https://doi.org/10.3389/FNHUM.2013.00413.

Cameron, C. D., Hutcherson, C. A., Ferguson, A. M., et al. (2019). Empathy is hard work: People choose to avoid empathy because of its cognitive costs. *Journal of Experimental Psychology: General, 148*(6), 962–976.

Carnap, R. (1995). Laws, Explanation, and Probability. In M. Gardne (Ed.), *An Introduction to the Philosophy of Science*. Dover Publications, pp. 3–39.

Cetinic, E., & She, J. (2022). Understanding and creating art with AI: Review and outlook. *ACM Transactions on Multimedia Computing, Communications, and Applications (TOMM), 18*(2), 1–22. https://doi.org/10.1145/3475799.

Chatel-Goldman, J., Congedo, M., Jutten, C., & Schwartz, J. L. (2014). Touch increases autonomic coupling between romantic partners. *Frontiers in Behavioral Neuroscience, 8*, 1–12. https://doi.org/10.3389/FNBEH.2014.00095.

Chakravarthula, S. N., Xiao, B., Imel, Z. E., Atkins, D. C., & Georgiou, P. G. (2015). Assessing empathy using static and dynamic behavior models based on therapist's language in addiction counseling. *Sixteenth Annual Conference of the International Speech Communication Association conference of the International Speech Communication Association*, pp. 669–672.

Chan, S., & Cassels, T. G. (2010). The role of culture in affective empathy cultural and bicultural differences. *Journal of Cognition and Culture, 10*(3–4), 309–326. https://doi.org/10.1163/156853710X531203

Chaudhary, K., Alam, M., Al-Rakhami, M. S., & Gumaei, A. (2021). Machine learning-based mathematical modelling for prediction of social media consumer behavior using big data analytics. *Journal of Big Data, 8*(1), 1–20.

Chen, K. H., Brown, C. L., Wells, J. L., et al. (2021). Physiological linkage during shared positive and shared negative emotion. *Journal of Personality and Social Psychology, 121*(5), 1029–1056. https://doi.org/10.1037/pspi0000337.

Cheng, Y., Chen, C., & Decety, J. (2017). How situational context impacts empathic responses and brain activation patterns. *Frontiers in Behavioral Neuroscience, 11*, 1–13. https://doi.org/10.3389/fnbeh.2017.00165.

Cheng, Y., Chen, C., Lin, C. P., Chou, K. H., & Decety, J. (2010). Love hurts: An fMRI study. *NeuroImage, 51*(2), 923–929. https://doi.org/10.1016/J.NEUROIMAGE.2010.02.047.

Cheng, Y., Lin, C. P., Liu, H. L., et al. (2007). Expertise modulates the perception of pain in others. *Current Biology, 17*(19), 1708–1713. https://doi.org/10.1016/j.cub.2007.09.020.

Cheng, Y., Yang, C. Y., Lin, C. P., Lee, P. L., & Decety, J. (2008). The perception of pain in others suppresses somatosensory oscillations: A magnetoencephalography study. *NeuroImage, 40*(4), 1833–1840. https://doi.org/10.1016/J.NEUROIMAGE.2008.01.064.

Chew, D., Tollit, M. A., Poulakis, Z., et al. (2020). Youths with a non-binary gender identity: A review of their sociodemographic and clinical profile. *The Lancet Child & Adolescent Health, 4*(4), 322–330.

Choshen-Hillel, S., Sadras, I., Gordon-Hecker, T., et al. (2022). Physicians prescribe fewer analgesics during night shifts than day shifts. *Proceedings of the National Academy of Sciences of the United States of America, 119*(27), 1–8. https://doi.org/10.1073/PNAS.2200047119.

Christov-Moore, L., Simpson, E. A., Coudé, G., et al. (2014). Empathy: Gender effects in brain and behavior. *Neuroscience & Biobehavioral Reviews, 46* (P4), 604–627. https://doi.org/10.1016/J.NEUBIOREV.2014.09.001.

Cikara, M., Bruneau, E. G., & Saxe, R. R. (2011). Us and them: Intergroup failures of empathy. *Current Directions in Psychological Science, 20*(3), 149–153. https://doi.org/10.1177/0963721411408713.

Clark, M. S., von Culin, K. R., Clark-Polner, E., & Lemay, E. P. (2017). Accuracy and projection in perceptions of partners' recent emotional experiences: Both minds matter. *Emotion, 17*(2), 196–207. https://doi.org/10.1037/EMO0000173.

Cohen, D., Landau, D. H., Friedman, D., et al. (2021). Exposure to social suffering in virtual reality boosts compassion and facial synchrony. *Computers in Human Behavior, 122*, 1–10. https://doi.org/10.1016/j.chb.2021.106781.

Coll, M. P. (2018). Meta-analysis of ERP investigations of pain empathy underlines methodological issues in ERP research. *Social Cognitive and Affective Neuroscience, 13*(10), 1003–1017. https://doi.org/10.1093/scan/nsy072.

Coll, M. P., Viding, E., Rütgen, M., et al. (2017). Are we really measuring empathy? Proposal for a new measurement framework. *Neuroscience & Biobehavioral Review, 83*, 132–139.

Contreras-Huerta, L. S., Baker, K. S., Reynolds, K. J., Batalha, L., & Cunnington, R. (2013). Racial bias in neural empathic responses to pain. *PLoS ONE, 8*(12), 1–10. https://doi.org/10.1371/JOURNAL.PONE.0084001.

Cordaro, D. T., Keltner, D., Tshering, S., Wangchuk, D., & Flynn, L. M. (2016). The voice conveys emotion in ten globalized cultures and one remote village in Bhutan. *Emotion, 16*(1), 117–128. https://doi.org/10.1037/EMO0000100.

Crivelli, C., & Fridlund, A. J. (2018). Facial displays are tools for social influence. *Trends in Cognitive Sciences*, *22*(5), 388–399. https://doi.org/10.1016/J.TICS.2018.02.006.

Cuff, B. M. P., Brown, S. J., Taylor, L., & Howat, D. J. (2016). Empathy: A review of the concept. *Emotion Review*, *8*(2), 144–153. https://doi.org/10.1177/1754073914558466.

Cui, F., Ma, N., & Luo, Y. J. (2016). Moral judgment modulates neural responses to the perception of other's pain: An ERP study. *Scientific Reports*, *6*, 1–8. https://doi.org/10.1038/srep20851.

Cui, F., Zhu, X., & Luo, Y. (2017). Social contexts modulate neural responses in the processing of others' pain: An event-related potential study. *Cognitive, Affective and Behavioral Neuroscience*, *17*(4), 850–857. https://doi.org/10.3758/s13415-017-0517-9.

Czeszumski, A., Eustergerling, S., Lang, A., et al. (2020). Hyperscanning: A valid method to study neural inter-brain underpinnings of social interaction. *Frontiers in Human Neuroscience*, *14*, 1–17. https://doi.org/10.3389/fnhum.2020.00039.

Czeszumski, A., Liang, S. H. Y., Dikker, S., et al. (2022). Cooperative behavior evokes interbrain synchrony in the prefrontal and temporoparietal cortex: A systematic review and meta-analysis of fNIRS hyperscanning studies. *Eneuro*, *9*(2), 1–9.

Dahl, T. S., & Boulos, M. N. K. (2013). Robots in health and social care: A complementary technology to home care and telehealthcare? *Robotics*, *3*(1), 1–21. https://doi.org/10.3390/ROBOTICS3010001.

Danziger, N., Prkachin, K. M., & Willer, J. C. (2006). Is pain the price of empathy? The perception of others' pain in patients with congenital insensitivity to pain. *Brain*, *129*(9), 2494–2507. https://doi.org/10.1093/brain/awl155.

Davis, M. H. (1983). Measuring individual differences in empathy: Evidence for a multidimensional approach. *Journal of Personality and Social Psychology*, *44*(1), 113–126.

de Corte, K., Buysse, A., Verhofstadt, L. L., et al. (2007). Measuring empathic tendencies: Reliability and validity of the Dutch version of the interpersonal reactivity index. *Psychologica Belgica*, *47*(4), 235–260. https://doi.org/10.5334/pb-47-4-235.

de Groot, J. H. B., Croijmans, I., & Smeets, M. A. M. (2020). More data, please: Machine learning to advance the multidisciplinary science of human sociochemistry. *Frontiers in Psychology*, *11*, 1–9. https://doi.org/10.3389/fpsyg.2020.581701.

de Groot, J. H. B., Smeets, M. A. M., Rowson, M. J., et al. (2015). A sniff of happiness. *Psychological Science, 26*(6), 684–700. https://doi.org/10.1177/0956797614566318.

de Vignemont, F., & Singer, T. (2006). The empathic brain: How, when and why? *Trends in Cognitive Sciences, 10*(10), 435–441. https://doi.org/10.1016/j.tics.2006.08.008.

de Waal, F. B. M. (2008). Putting the altruism back into altruism: The evolution of empathy. *Annual Review of Psychology, 59*, 279–300. https://doi.org/10.1146/ANNUREV.PSYCH.59.103006.093625.

de Waal, F. B. M., & Preston, S. D. (2017). Mammalian empathy: Behavioural manifestations and neural basis. *Nature Reviews Neuroscience, 18*(8), 498–509. https://doi.org/10.1038/nrn.2017.72

Decety, J. (2020). Empathy in medicine: What it is, and how much we really need it. *American Journal of Medicine, 133*(5), 561–566. https://doi.org/10.1016/j.amjmed.2019.12.012.

Decety, J. (2021). Why empathy is not a reliable source of information in moral decision making. *Current Directions in Psychological Science, 30*(5), 425–430. https://doi.org/10.1177/09637214211031943.

Decety, J., & Jackson, P. L. (2004). The functional architecture of human empathy. *Behavioral and Cognitive Neuroscience Reviews, 3*(2), 71–100. https://doi.org/10.1177/1534582304267187.

Decety, J., Yang, C. Y., & Cheng, Y. (2010). Physicians down-regulate their pain empathy response: An event-related brain potential study. *NeuroImage, 50*(4), 1676–1682. https://doi.org/10.1016/j.neuroimage.2010.01.025.

Demurie, E., de Corel, M., & Roeyers, H. (2011). Empathic accuracy in adolescents with autism spectrum disorders and adolescents with attention-deficit/hyperactivity disorder. *Research in Autism Spectrum Disorders, 5*(1), 126–134. https://doi.org/10.1016/J.RASD.2010.03.002.

Depow, G. J., Francis, Z., & Inzlicht, M. (2021). The experience of empathy in everyday life. *Psychological Science, 32*(8), 1198–1213. https://doi.org/10.1177/0956797621995202.

Derntl, B., Finkelmeyer, A., Toygar, T. K., et al. (2009). Generalized deficit in all core components of empathy in schizophrenia. *Schizophrenia Research, 108*(1–3), 197–206. https://doi.org/10.1016/J.SCHRES.2008.11.009.

Deuter, C. E., Nowacki, J., Wingenfeld, K., et al. (2018). The role of physiological arousal for self-reported emotional empathy. *Autonomic Neuroscience, 214*, 9–14. https://doi.org/10.1016/J.AUTNEU.2018.07.002.

Diamond, L. M. (2020). Gender fluidity and nonbinary gender identities among children and adolescents. *Child Development Perspectives, 14*(2), 110–115.

DiGirolamo, M. A., Simon, J. C., Hubley, K. M., Kopulsky, A., & Gutsell, J. N. (2019). Clarifying the relationship between trait empathy and action-based resonance indexed by EEG mu-rhythm suppression. *Neuropsychologia, 133*, 1–12. https://doi.org/10.1016/J.NEUROPSYCHOLOGIA.2019.107172.

Dor-Ziderman, Y., Cohen, D., Levit-Binnun, N., & Golland, Y. (2021). Synchrony with distress in affective empathy and compassion. *Psychophysiology, 58*(10), 1–16. https://doi.org/10.1111/psyp.13889.

Drimalla, H., Landwehr, N., Hess, U., & Dziobek, I. (2019). From face to face: The contribution of facial mimicry to cognitive and emotional empathy. *Cognition and Emotion*, 1672–1686.

Duan, H., Wang, Y. J., & Lei, X. (2021). The effect of sleep deprivation on empathy for pain: An ERP study. *Neuropsychologia, 163*, 1–9. https://doi.org/10.1016/J.NEUROPSYCHOLOGIA.2021.108084.

Duda, R. O., Hart, P. E., & Stork, D. G. (2012). *Pattern Classification.* John Wiley.

Dumas, G., Nadel, J., Soussignan, R., Martinerie, J., & Garnero, L. (2010). Inter-brain synchronization during social interaction. *PLoS ONE, 5*(8), 1–10. https://doi.org/10.1371/journal.pone.0012166.

Dziobek, I., Rogers, K., Fleck, S., et al. (2008). Dissociation of cognitive and emotional empathy in adults with Asperger syndrome using the Multifaceted Empathy Test (MET). *Journal of Autism and Developmental Disorders, 38* (3), 464–473. https://doi.org/10.1007/S10803-007-0486-X.

Eisenberg, N., & Fabes, R. A. (1990). Empathy: Conceptualization, measurement, and relation to prosocial behavior. *Motivation and Emotion, 14*(2), 131–149. https://doi.org/10.1007/BF00991640.

Eisenberg, N., & Lennon, R. (1983). Sex differences in empathy and related capacities. *Psychological Bulletin, 94*(1), 100–131. https://doi.org/10.1037/0033-2909.94.1.100.

Ekman, P., Friesen, W., & Ellsworth, P. (1972). *Emotion in the Human Face: Guidelines for Research and an Integration of Findings: Guidelines for Research and an Integration of Findings.* Pergamon.

Epley, N., & Eyal, T. (2019). Through a looking glass, darkly: Using mechanisms of mind perception to identify accuracy, overconfidence, and underappreciated means for improvement. In J. M. Olsen (Ed.), *Advances in Experimental Social Psychology* (Vol. 60). Academic Press, pp. 65–120. https://doi.org/10.1016/bs.aesp.2019.04.002.

Epley, N., Keysar, B., van Boven, L., & Gilovich, T. (2004). Perspective taking as egocentric anchoring and adjustment. *Article in Journal of Personality and Social Psychology, 87*(3), 327–339. https://doi.org/10.1037/0022-3514.87.3.327.

Eyal, T., Steffel, M., & Epley, N. (2018). Perspective mistaking: Accurately understanding the mind of another requires getting perspective, not taking perspective. *Journal of Personality and Social Psychology, 114*(4), 547–571. https://doi.org/10.1037/PSPA0000115.

Eysenbach, G. (2023). The role of chatgpt, generative language models, and artificial intelligence in medical education: A conversation with chatgpt and a call for papers. *JMIR Medical Education, 9*(1), 1–13.

Fabi, S., & Leuthold, H. (2017). Empathy for pain influences perceptual and motor processing: Evidence from response force, ERPs, and EEG oscillations. *Social Neuroscience, 12*(6), 701–716. https://doi.org/10.1080/17470919.2016.1238009.

Fallon, N., Roberts, C., & Stancak, A. (2020). Shared and distinct functional networks for empathy and pain processing: A systematic review and meta-analysis of fMRI studies. *Social Cognitive and Affective Neuroscience, 15*(7), 709–723. https://doi.org/10.1093/scan/nsaa090.

Fan, Y., Duncan, N. W., de Greck, M., & Northoff, G. (2011). Is there a core neural network in empathy? An fMRI based quantitative meta-analysis. *Neuroscience and Biobehavioral Reviews, 35*(3), 903–911. https://doi.org/10.1016/j.neubiorev.2010.10.009.

Fan, Y., & Han, S. (2008). Temporal dynamic of neural mechanisms involved in empathy for pain: An event-related brain potential study. *Neuropsychologia, 46*(1), 160–173. https://doi.org/10.1016/j.neuropsychologia.2007.07.023.

Feldman, R., Magori-Cohen, R., Galili, G., Singer, M., & Louzoun, Y. (2011). Mother and infant coordinate heart rhythms through episodes of interaction synchrony. *Infant Behavior and Development, 34*(4), 569–577. https://doi.org/10.1016/J.INFBEH.2011.06.008.

FeldmanHall, O., Dalgleish, T., Evans, D., & Mobbs, D. (2015). Empathic concern drives costly altruism. *NeuroImage, 105*, 347–356. https://doi.org/10.1016/j.neuroimage.2014.10.043.

Feng, C., Li, Z., Feng, X., et al. (2016). Social hierarchy modulates neural responses of empathy for pain. *Social Cognitive and Affective Neuroscience, 11*(3), 485–495. https://doi.org/10.1093/scan/nsv135.

Ferguson, A. M., Cameron, C. D., & Inzlicht, M. (2020). Motivational effects on empathic choices. *Journal of Experimental Social Psychology, 90*, 1–17.

Fourie, M. M., Subramoney, S., Gobodo- Madikizela, P. (2017). A less attractive feature of empathy: Intergroup empathy bias. In *Empathy – An Evidence-Based Interdisciplinary Perspective*. IntechOpen, pp. 45–61. https://doi.org/10.5772/INTECHOPEN.69287.

Fox, N. A., Yoo, K. H., Bowman, L. C., et al. (2016). Assessing human mirror activity with EEG mu rhythm: A meta-analysis. *Psychological Bulletin, 142*(3), 291–313. https://doi.org/10.1037/BUL0000031.

Fridenson-Hayo, S., Berggren, S., Lassalle, A., et al. (2016). Basic and complex emotion recognition in children with autism: Cross-cultural findings. *Molecular Autism, 7*(1), 1–11. https://doi.org/10.1186/S13229-016-0113-9.

Fusaro, M., Tieri, G., & Aglioti, S. M. (2016). Seeing pain and pleasure on self and others: Behavioural and psychophysiological reactivity in immersive virtual reality. *Journal of Neurophysiology, 116*(6), 2656–2662. https://doi.org/10.1152/JN.00489.2016.

Gantiva, C., Araujo, A., Castillo, K., Claro, L., & Hurtado-Parrado, C. (2021). Physiological and affective responses to emoji faces: Effects on facial muscle activity, skin conductance, heart rate, and self-reported affect. *Biological Psychology, 163*, 1–6. https://doi.org/10.1016/J.BIOPSYCHO.2021.108142.

Gelstein, S., Yeshurun, Y., Rozenkrantz, L., et al. (2011). Human tears contain a chemosignal. *Science, 331*(6014), 226–230. https://doi.org/10.1126/SCIENCE.1198331.

Gendron, M., Roberson, D., van der Vyver, J. M., & Barrett, L. F. (2014). Cultural relativity in perceiving emotion from vocalizations. *Psychological Science, 25*(4), 911–920. https://doi.org/10.1177/0956797613517239.

Genzer, S., Ong, D. C., Zaki, J., & Perry, A. (2022). Mu rhythm suppression over sensorimotor regions is associated with greater empathic accuracy. *Social Cognitive and Affective Neuroscience, 17*(9), 788–801. https://doi.org/10.1093/SCAN/NSAC011.

Gesn, P. R., & Ickes, W. (1999). The development of meaning contexts for empathic accuracy: Channel and sequence effects. *Journal of Personality and Social Psychology, 77*(4), 746–761. https://doi.org/10.1037/0022-3514.77.4.746.

Gibson, J., Malandrakis, N., Romero, F., Atkins, D. C., & Narayanan, S. (2015). Predicting therapist empathy in motivational interviews using language features inspired by psycholinguistic norms. *Sixteenth Annual Conference of the International Speech Communication Association*, pp. 1947–1951.

Gleichgerrcht, E., Torralva, T., Rattazzi, A., et al. (2013). Selective impairment of cognitive empathy for moral judgment in adults with high functioning autism. *Social Cognitive and Affective Neuroscience, 8*(7), 780–788. https://doi.org/10.1093/SCAN/NSS067.

Goel, S., Jara-Ettinger, J., & Gendron, M. (2022). Modeling cue-integration in emotion inferences. *Proceedings of the Annual Meeting of the Cognitive Science Society, 44*(44), 862–868.

Goldman, A. I. (2006). *Simulating Minds: The Philosophy, Psychology, and Neuroscience of Mindreading*. Oxford University Press on Demand.

Goldstein, P., Weissman-Fogel, I., Dumas, G., & Shamay-Tsoory, S. G. (2018). Brain-to-brain coupling during handholding is associated with pain reduction.

Proceedings of the National Academy of Sciences of the United States of America, 115(11), E2528–E2537. https://doi.org/10.1073/PNAS.1703643115.

Goldstein, P., Weissman-Fogel, I., & Shamay-Tsoory, S. G. (2017). The role of touch in regulating inter-partner physiological coupling during empathy for pain. *Scientific Reports, 7*(1), 1–12. https://doi.org/10.1038/s41598-017-03627-7.

Golland, Y., Arzouan, Y., & Levit-Binnun, N. (2015). The mere co-presence: Synchronization of autonomic signals and emotional responses across co-present individuals not engaged in direct interaction. *PLoS ONE, 10*(5), 1–13. https://doi.org/10.1371/JOURNAL.PONE.0125804.

Gomez, P., Stahel, W. A., & Danuser, B. (2004). Respiratory responses during affective picture viewing. *Biological Psychology, 67*(3), 359–373. https://doi.org/10.1016/J.BIOPSYCHO.2004.03.013.

Graham, T., & Ickes, W. (1997). When women's intuition isn't greater than men's. In W. Ickes (Ed.), *Empathic Accuracy.* Guilford, pp. 117–143. https://psycnet.apa.org/record/1997-97352-004.

Grant, B. J., Fetterman, Z., Weyhaupt, M. B., Kim, M., & Tullett, A. M. (2018). It takes two: A replication. *Journal of Research in Personality, 72*, 58–63. https://doi.org/10.1016/J.JRP.2016.06.023.

Green, M. F., Bearden, C. E., Cannon, T. D., et al. (2012). Social cognition in schizophrenia, Part 1: Performance across phase of illness. *Schizophrenia Bulletin, 38*(4), 854–864. https://doi.org/10.1093/SCHBUL/SBQ171.

Green, M. F., Olivier, B., Crawley, J. N., Penn, D. L., & Silverstein, S. (2005). Social cognition in schizophrenia: Recommendations from the measurement and treatment research to improve cognition in schizophrenia new approaches conference. *Schizophrenia Bulletin, 31*(4), 882–887. https://doi.org/10.1093/SCHBUL/SBI049.

Grove, R., Baillie, A., Allison, C., Baron-Cohen, S., & Hoekstra, R. A. (2014). The latent structure of cognitive and emotional empathy in individuals with autism, first-degree relatives and typical individuals. *Molecular Autism, 5*(1), 1–10. https://doi.org/10.1186/2040-2392-5-42.

Grynberg, D., & Konrath, S. (2020). The closer you feel, the more you care: Positive associations between closeness, pain intensity rating, empathic concern and personal distress to someone in pain. *Acta Psychologica, 210*, 1–7. https://doi.org/10.1016/j.actpsy.2020.103175.

Gu, X., & Han, S. (2007). Attention and reality constraints on the neural processes of empathy for pain. *NeuroImage, 36*(1), 256–267. https://doi.org/10.1016/j.neuroimage.2007.02.025.

Guhn, A., Merkel, L., Hübner, L., et al. (2020). Understanding versus feeling the emotions of others: How persistent and recurrent depression affect empathy. *Journal of Psychiatric Research*, *130*, 120–127. https://doi.org/10.1016/J.JPSYCHIRES.2020.06.023.

Guo, X., Zheng, L., Wang, H., et al. (2013). Exposure to violence reduces empathetic responses to other's pain. *Brain and Cognition*, *82*(2), 187–191. https://doi.org/10.1016/j.bandc.2013.04.005.

Guo, X., Zheng, L., Zhang, W., et al. (2012). Empathic neural responses to others' pain depend on monetary reward. *Social Cognitive and Affective Neuroscience*, *7*(5), 535–541. https://doi.org/10.1093/scan/nsr034.

Gutsell, J. N., Simon, J. C., & Jiang, Y. (2020). Perspective taking reduces group biases in sensorimotor resonance. *Cortex*, *131*, 42–53. https://doi.org/10.1016/J.CORTEX.2020.04.037.

Hajcak, G., & Foti, D. (2020). Significance? . . . significance! empirical, methodological, and theoretical connections between the late positive potential and P300 as neural responses to stimulus significance: An integrative review. *Psychophysiology*, *57*(7), 1–15. https://doi.org/10.1111/PSYP.13570.

Hajcak, G., Macnamara, A., & Olvet, D. M. (2010). Event-related potentials, emotion, and emotion regulation: An integrative review. *Developmental Neuropsychology*, *35*(2), 129–155. https://doi.org/10.1080/87565640903526504.

Hall, J. A. (1978). Gender effects in decoding nonverbal cues. *Psychological Bulletin*, *85*(4), 845–857. https://doi.org/10.1037/0033-2909.85.4.845.

Hall, J. A., & Schmid Mast, M. (2007). Sources of accuracy in the empathic accuracy paradigm. *Emotion*, *7*(2), 438–446. https://doi.org/10.1037/1528-3542.7.2.438.

Hall, J. A., & Schwartz, R. (2019). Empathy present and future. *Journal of Social Psychology*, *159*(3), 225–243. https://doi.org/10.1080/00224545.2018.1477442.

Han, S. (2018). Neurocognitive basis of racial ingroup bias in empathy. *Trends in Cognitive Sciences*, *22*(5), 400–421. https://doi.org/10.1016/j.tics.2018.02.013.

Hartmann, H., Forbes, P., Rutgen, M., & Lamm, C. (2022). Placebo analgesia reduces costly prosocial helping to lower another's pain. *Psychological Science*, *33*(11), 1881–1867.

Hasson, Y., Amir, E., Sobol-Sarag, D., Tamir, M., & Halperin, E. (2022). Using performance art to promote intergroup prosociality by cultivating the belief that empathy is unlimited. *Nature Communications*, *13*(1), 1–15.

Hasson, U., Ghazanfar, A. A., Galantucci, B., Garrod, S., & Keysers, C. (2012). Brain-to-brain coupling: A mechanism for creating and sharing a social world. *Trends in Cognitive Sciences*, *16*(2), 114–121. https://doi.org/10.1016/J.TICS.2011.12.007.

Hawk, S. T., van Kleef, G. A., Fischer, A. H., & van der Schalk, J. (2009). "Worth a thousand words": Absolute and relative decoding of nonlinguistic affect vocalizations. *Emotion, 9*(3), 293–305. https://doi.org/10.1037/A0015178.

Hein, G., Lamm, C., Brodbeck, C., & Singer, T. (2011). Skin conductance response to the pain of others predicts later costly helping. *PLoS ONE, 6* (8), 1–6. https://doi.org/10.1371/JOURNAL.PONE.0022759.

Hein, G., Silani, G., Preuschoff, K., Batson, C. D., & Singer, T. (2010). Neural responses to ingroup and outgroup members' suffering predict individual differences in costly helping. *Neuron, 68*(1), 149–160. https://doi.org/10.1016/j.neuron.2010.09.003.

Henrich, J., Heine, S. J., & Norenzayan, A. (2010). Most people are not WEIRD. *Nature, 466*(7302), 29.

Herbert, C., Junghofer, M., & Kissler, J. (2008). Event related potentials to emotional adjectives during reading. *Psychophysiology, 45*(3), 487–498. https://doi.org/10.1111/J.1469-8986.2007.00638.X.

Herrera, F., Bailenson, J., Weisz, E., Ogle, E., & Zak, J. (2018). Building long-term empathy: A large-scale comparison of traditional and virtual reality perspective-taking. *PLoS ONE, 13*(10), 1–37. https://doi.org/10.1371/journal.pone.0204494.

Hillman, E. M. (2014). Coupling mechanism and significance of the BOLD signal: A status report. *Annual Review of Neuroscience, 37,* 161–181.

Ho, F., & Mussap, A. J. (2019). The gender identity scale: Adapting the gender unicorn to measure gender identity. *Psychology of Sexual Orientation and Gender Diversity, 6*(2), 217–231.

Hobson, H. M., & Bishop, D. V. M. (2017). The interpretation of mu suppression as an index of mirror neuron activity: Past, present and future. *Royal Society Open Science, 4*(3), 1–22. https://doi.org/10.1098/rsos.160662.

Hoenen, M., Lübke, K. T., & Pause, B. M. (2015). Somatosensory mu activity reflects imagined pain intensity of others. *Psychophysiology, 52*(12), 1551–1558. https://doi.org/10.1111/psyp.12522.

Hoenen, M., Lübke, K. T., & Pause, B. M. (2018). Empathic cognitions affected by undetectable social chemosignals: An EEG study on visually evoked empathy for pain in an auditory and chemosensory context. *Frontiers in Behavioral Neuroscience, 12,* 1–14. https://doi.org/10.3389/fnbeh.2018.00243.

Hoenen, M., Schain, C., & Pause, B. M. (2013). Down-modulation of mu-activity through empathic top-down processes. *Social Neuroscience, 8* (5), 515–524. https://doi.org/10.1080/17470919.2013.833550.

Hofer, M. K., Chen, F. S., & Schaller, M. (2020). What your nose knows: Affective, cognitive, and behavioral responses to the scent of another person.

Current Directions in Psychological Science, 29(6), 617–623. https://doi.org/ 10.1177/0963721420964175.

Holding, B. C., Sundelin, T., Lekander, M., & Axelsson, J. (2019). Sleep deprivation and its effects on communication during individual and collaborative tasks. *Scientific Reports, 9*(1), 1–8. https://doi.org/10.1038/s41598-019-39271-6.

Horan, W. P., & Green, M. F. (2019). Treatment of social cognition in schizophrenia: Current status and future directions. *Schizophrenia Research, 203*, 3–11. https://doi.org/10.1016/J.SCHRES.2017.07.013.

Howland, M., & Rafaeli, E. (2010). Bringing everyday mind reading into everyday life: Assessing empathic accuracy with daily diary data. *Journal of Personality, 78*(5), 1437–1468. https://doi.org/10.1111/J.1467-6494.2010.00657.X.

Hu, Y., Pan, Y., Shi, X., et al. (2018). Inter-brain synchrony and cooperation context in interactive decision making. *Biological Psychology, 133*, 54–62. https://doi.org/10.1016/J.BIOPSYCHO.2017.12.005.

Ickes, W., Stinson, L., Bissonnette, V., & Garcia, S. (1990). Naturalistic social cognition: Empathic accuracy in mixed-sex dyads. *Journal of Personality and Social Psychology, 59*(4), 730–742. https://doi.org/10.1037/0022-3514.59.4.730.

Indolia, S., Goswami, A. K., Mishra, S. P., & Asopa, P. (2018). Conceptual understanding of convolutional neural network- A deep learning approach. *Procedia Computer Science, 132*, 679–688. https://doi.org/10.1016/J.PROCS.2018.05.069.

Ionta, S., Costantini, M., Ferretti, A., et al. (2020). Visual similarity and psychological closeness are neurally dissociable in the brain response to vicarious pain. *Cortex, 133*, 295–308. https://doi.org/10.1016/j.cortex.2020.09.028.

Ishida, H., Suzuki, K., & Grandi, L. C. (2015). Predictive coding accounts of shared representations in parieto-insular networks. *Neuropsychologia, 70*, 442–454. https://doi.org/10.1016/J.NEUROPSYCHOLOGIA.2014.10.020.

Israelashvili, J., Oosterwijk, S., Sauter, D., & Fischer, A. (2019). Knowing me, knowing you: Emotion differentiation in oneself is associated with recognition of others' emotions. *Cognition and Emotion, 33*(7), 1461–1471. https://doi.org/10.1080/02699931.2019.1577221.

Israelashvili, J., & Perry, A. (2021). Nuancing perspective: Feedback shapes the understanding of another's emotions. *Social Psychology, 52*(4), 238–249. https://doi.org/10.1027/1864-9335/A000452.

Israelashvili, J., Sauter, D., & Fischer, A. (2020). Two facets of affective empathy: Concern and distress have opposite relationships to emotion recognition. *Cognition and Emotion*, *34*(6), 1112–1122. https://doi.org/10.1080/02699931.2020.1724893.

Jack, R. E., Garrod, O. G. B., Yu, H., Caldara, R., & Schyns, P. G. (2012). Facial expressions of emotion are not culturally universal. *Proceedings of the National Academy of Sciences of the United States of America*, *109*(19), 7241–7244. https://doi.org/10.1073/PNAS.1200155109.

Jackson, P. L., Meltzoff, A. N., & Decety, J. (2005). How do we perceive the pain of others? A window into the neural processes involved in empathy. *NeuroImage*, *24*(3), 771–779. https://doi.org/10.1016/j.neuroimage.2004.09.006.

Jamali, M., Grannan, B. L., Fedorenko, E., et al. (2021). Single-neuronal predictions of others' beliefs in humans. *Nature*, *591*, 610–614. https://doi.org/10.1038/s41586-021-03184-0.

Jami, P. Y., Walker, D. I., & Mansouri, B. (2023). Interaction of empathy and culture: A review. *Current Psychology*, 1–16.

Jolliffe, D., & Farrington, D. P. (2004). Empathy and offending: A systematic review and meta-analysis. *Aggression and Violent Behavior*, *9*(5), 441–476. https://doi.org/10.1016/J.AVB.2003.03.001.

Jones, A. P., Happé, F. G. E., Gilbert, F., Burnett, S., & Viding, E. (2010). Feeling, caring, knowing: Different types of empathy deficit in boys with psychopathic tendencies and autism spectrum disorder. *Journal of Child Psychology and Psychiatry*, *51*(11), 1188–1197. https://doi.org/10.1111/J.1469-7610.2010.02280.X.

Jospe, K., Genzer, S., klein Selle, N., Ong, D., Zaki, J., & Perry, A. (2020). The contribution of linguistic and visual cues to physiological synchrony and empathic accuracy. *Cortex*, *132*, 296–308. https://doi.org/10.1016/j.cortex.2020.09.001.

Jospe, K., Genzer, S., Mansano, L., et al. (2022). Impaired empathic accuracy following damage to the left hemisphere. *Biological Psychology*, *172*, 1–12. https://doi.org/10.1016/J.BIOPSYCHO.2022.108380.

Joyal, C. C., Neveu, S. M., Boukhalfi, T., Jackson, P. L., & Renaud, P. (2018). Suppression of sensorimotor alpha power associated with pain expressed by an avatar: A preliminary EEG study. *Frontiers in Human Neuroscience*, *12*, 1–7. https://doi.org/10.3389/fnhum.2018.00273.

Keltner, D., Sauter, D., Tracy, J., & Cowen, A. (2019). Emotional expression: Advances in basic emotion theory. *Journal of Nonverbal Behavior*, *43*(2), 133–160. https://doi.org/10.1007/S10919-019-00293-3.

Keysers, C., & Gazzola, V. (2014). Dissociating the ability and propensity for empathy. *Trends in Cognitive Sciences*, *18*(4), 163–166.

Keysers, C., & Gazzola, V. (2017). Plea for cross-species social neuroscience. In M. Wöhr & S. Krach (Eds.), *Social Behavior from Rodents to Humans*. Springer, pp. 179–191.

Keysers, C., Wicker, B., Gazzola, V., et al. (2004). A touching sight: SII/PV activation during the observation and experience of touch. *Neuron, 42,* 335–346.

Kilner, J. M., Friston, K. J., & Frith, C. D. (2007). Predictive coding: An account of the mirror neuron system. *Cognitive Processing, 8*(3), 159–166. https://doi.org/10.1007/S10339-007-0170-2.

Kirkland, R., Peterson, E., Baker, C., & Pulos, S. (2013). Meta-analysis reveals adult female superiority in "reading the mind in the eyes test." *North American Journal of Psychology, 15*(1), 121–146. www.researchgate.net/publication/260712981.

Kitayama, S., Duffy, S., Kawamura, T., & Larsen, J. T. (2003). Perceiving an object and its context in different cultures: A cultural look at new look. *Psychological Science, 14*(3), 201–206. https://doi.org/10.1111/1467-9280.02432.

Klein, K. J. K., & Hodges, S. D. (2001). Gender differences, motivation, and empathic accuracy: When it pays to understand. *Personality and Social Psychology Bulletin, 27*(6), 720–730. https://doi.org/10.1177/0146167201276007.

Kliemann, D., & Adolphs, R. (2018). The social neuroscience of mentalizing: Challenges and recommendations. *Current Opinion in Psychology, 24,* 1–6. https://doi.org/10.1016/J.COPSYC.2018.02.015.

Kogler, L., Müller, V. I., Werminghausen, E., Eickhoff, S. B., & Derntl, B. (2020). Do I feel or do I know? Neuroimaging meta-analyses on the multiple facets of empathy. *Cortex, 129,* 341–355. https://doi.org/10.1016/j.cortex.2020.04.031.

Kohler, C. G., Walker, J. B., Martin, E. A., Healey, K. M., & Moberg, P. J. (2010). Facial emotion perception in schizophrenia: A meta-analytic review. *Schizophrenia Bulletin, 36*(5), 1009–1019. https://doi.org/10.1093/SCHBUL/SBN192.

Kosonogov, V., de Zorzi, L., Honoré, J., et al. (2017). Facial thermal variations: A new marker of emotional arousal. *PLoS ONE, 12*(9), 1–15. https://doi.org/10.1371/JOURNAL.PONE.0183592.

Koster, J., Leckie, G., & Aven, B. (2019). Statistical methods and software for the multilevel social relations model. *Field Methods, 32*(4), 339–345. https://doi.org/10.1177/1525822X19889011.

Krach, S., Cohrs, J. C., de Echeverría Loebell, N. C., et al. (2011). Your flaws are my pain: Linking empathy to vicarious embarrassment. *PLoS ONE, 6*(4). https://doi.org/10.1371/journal.pone.0018675.

Kraus, M. W., Côté, S., & Keltner, D. (2010). Social class, contextualism, and empathic accuracy. *Psychological Science, 21*(11), 1716–1723.

Kreibig, S. D. (2010). Autonomic nervous system activity in emotion: A review. *Biological Psychology, 84*, 14–41. https://doi.org/10.1016/j.biopsycho.2010.03.010.

Kreibig, S. D., Wilhelm, F. H., Roth, W. T., & Gross, J. J. (2007). Cardiovascular, electrodermal, and respiratory response patterns to fear- and sadness-inducing films. *Psychophysiology, 44*(5), 787–806. https://doi.org/10.1111/J.1469-8986.2007.00550.X.

Kyle, S. D., Beattie, L., Spiegelhalder, K., Rogers, Z., & Espie, C. A. (2014). Altered emotion perception in insomnia disorder. *Sleep, 37*(4), 775–783. https://doi.org/10.5665/SLEEP.3588.

Lamm, C., Batson, C. D., & Decety, J. (2007). The neural substrate of human empathy: Effects of perspective-taking and cognitive appraisal. *Journal of Cognitive Neuroscience, 19*(1), 42–58. https://doi.org/10.1162/jocn.2007.19.1.42.

Lamm, C., Bukowski, H., & Silani, G. (2016). From shared to distinct self-other representations in empathy: Evidence from neurotypical function and socio-cognitive disorders. *Philosophical Transactions of the Royal Society B: Biological Sciences, 371*(1686), 1–7. https://doi.org/10.1098/rstb.2015.0083.

Lamm, C., Decety, J., & Singer, T. (2011). Meta-analytic evidence for common and distinct neural networks associated with directly experienced pain and empathy for pain. *NeuroImage, 54*(3), 2492–2502. https://doi.org/10.1016/j.neuroimage.2010.10.014.

Lamm, C., & Majdandžić, J. (2015). The role of shared neural activations, mirror neurons, and morality in empathy: A critical comment. *Neuroscience Research, 90*, 15–24. https://doi.org/10.1016/j.neures.2014.10.008.

Lamm, C., Nausbaum, H. C., Meltzoff, A. N., & Decety, J. (2007). What are you feeling? Using functional magnetic resonance imaging to assess the modulation of sensory and affective responses during empathy for pain. *PLoS ONE, 2*(12), 1–16. https://doi.org/10.1371/journal.pone.0001292.

Lamm, C., Rütgen, M., & Wagner, I. C. (2019). Imaging empathy and prosocial emotions. *Neuroscience Letters, 693*, 49–53. https://doi.org/10.1016/j.neulet.2017.06.054.

Lange, J., Heerdink, M. W., & van Kleef, G. A. (2022). Reading emotions, reading people: Emotion perception and inferences drawn from perceived emotions. *Current Opinion in Psychology, 43*, 85–90. https://doi.org/10.1016/J.COPSYC.2021.06.008.

Laukka, P., & Elfenbein, H. A. (2021). Cross-cultural emotion recognition and in-group advantage in vocal expression: A meta-analysis. *Emotion Review*, *13*(1), 3–11. https://doi.org/10.1177/1754073919897295.

Laukka, P., Thingujam, N. S., Iraki, F. K., et al. (2016). The expression and recognition of emotions in the voice across five nations: A lens model analysis based on acoustic features. *Journal of Personality and Social Psychology*, *111*(5), 686–705. https://doi.org/10.1037/PSPI0000066.

Lecker, M., & Aviezer, H. (2021). More than words? Semantic emotion labels boost context effects on faces. *Affective Science*, *2*(2), 163–170.

Lecker, M., Dotsch, R., Bijlstra, G., & Aviezer, H. (2020). Bidirectional contextual influence between faces and bodies in emotion perception. *Emotion*, *20*(7), 1154–1164.

Lehmann, K., Böckler, A., Klimecki, O., Müller-Liebmann, C., & Kanske, P. (2022). Empathy and correct mental state inferences both promote prosociality. *Scientific Reports*, *12*(1), 1–8. https://doi.org/10.1038/s41598-022-20855-8.

Levenson, R. W., & Gottman, J. M. (1983). Marital interaction: Physiological linkage and affective exchange. *Journal of Personality and Social Psychology*, *45*(3), 587–597. https://doi.org/10.1037/0022-3514.45.3.587.

Levenson, R. W., & Ruef, A. M. (1992). Empathy: A physiological substrate. *Journal of Personality and Social Psychology*, *63*(2), 234–246. https://doi.org/10.1037/0022-3514.63.2.234.

Levy, J., Goldstein, A., & Feldman, R. (2017). Perception of social synchrony induces mother–child gamma coupling in the social brain. *Social Cognitive and Affective Neuroscience*, *12*(7), 1036–1046. https://doi.org/10.1093/SCAN/NSX032.

Levy, J., Goldstein, A., Influs, M., et al. (2016). Adolescents growing up amidst intractable conflict attenuate brain response to pain of outgroup. *Proceedings of the National Academy of Sciences of the United States of America*, *113*(48), 13696–13701. https://doi.org/10.1073/PNAS.1612903113.

Li, X., Liu, Y., Ye, Q., Lu, X., & Peng, W. (2020). The linkage between first-hand pain sensitivity and empathy for others' pain: Attention matters. *Human Brain Mapping*, *41*(17), 4815–4828. https://doi.org/10.1002/hbm.25160.

Liu, D., Liu, S., Liu, X., et al. (2018). Interactive brain activity: Review and progress on EEG-based hyperscanning in social interactions. *Frontiers in Psychology*, *9*, 1–11. https://doi.org/10.3389/fpsyg.2018.01862.

Lobchuk, M., Halas, G., West, C., et al. (2016). Development of a novel empathy-related video-feedback intervention to improve empathic accuracy of nursing students: A pilot study. *Nurse Education Today*, *46*, 86–93.

Loggia, M. L., Mogil, J. S., & Bushnell, M. C. (2008). Empathy hurts: Compassion for another increases both sensory and affective components of pain perception. *Pain, 136*(1–2), 168–176. https://doi.org/10.1016/j .pain.2007.07.017.

Logothetis, N. K. (2008). What we can do and what we cannot do with fMRI. *Nature, 453*(7197), 869–878.

Logothetis, N. K., Pauls, J., Augath, M., Trinath, T., & Oeltermann, A. (2001). Neurophysiological investigation of the basis of the fMRI signal. *Nature, 412* (6843), 150–157.

López-Solà, M., Koban, L., Krishnan, A., & Wager, T. D. (2020). When pain really matters: A vicarious-pain brain marker tracks empathy for pain in the romantic partner. *Neuropsychologia, 145*, 1–8. https://doi.org/10.1016/j .neuropsychologia.2017.07.012.

Mackes, N. K., Golm, D., O'Daly, O. G., et al. (2018). Tracking emotions in the brain – Revisiting the Empathic Accuracy Task. *NeuroImage, 178*, 677–686. https://doi.org/10.1016/j.neuroimage.2018.05.080.

Marangoni, C., Garcia, S., Ickes, W., & Teng, G. (1995). Empathic accuracy in a clinically relevant setting. *Journal of Personality and Social Psychology*, 68 (5), 854–869.

Markus, H. R., & Kitayama, S. (1991). Culture and the self: Implications for cognition, emotion, and motivation. *Psychological Review, 98*(2), 224–253. https://doi.org/10.1037/0033-295X.98.2.224.

Marsella, S., & Gratch, J. (2014). Computationally modeling human emotion. *Communications of the ACM, 57*(12), 56–67. https://doi.org/10.1145/ 2631912.

Marsh, A. A. (2022). Comment: Getting our affect together: Shared representations as the core of empathy. *Emotion Review, 14*(3), 184–187. https://doi .org/10.1177/17540739221107029.

Mayo, O., Lavidor, M., & Gordon, I. (2021). Interpersonal autonomic nervous system synchrony and its association to relationship and performance: A systematic review and meta-analysis. *Physiology and Behavior, 235*, 1–11. https://doi.org/10.1016/j.physbeh.2021.113391.

McClure, E. B. (2000). A meta-analytic review of sex differences in facial expression processing and their development in infants, children, and adolescents. *Psychological Bulletin, 126*(3), 424–453. https://doi.org/ 10.1037/0033-2909.126.3.424.

MCDonald, B., Bockler, A., & Kanske, P. (2022). Soundtrack to the social world: Emotional music enhances empathy, compassion, and prosocial decisions but not theory of mind. *Emotion, 22*(1), 19–29. https://doi.org/10.1037/ emo0001036.

Melloni, M., Lopez, V., & Ibanez, A. (2014). Empathy and contextual social cognition. *Cognitive, Affective and Behavioral Neuroscience, 14*(1), 407–425. https://doi.org/10.3758/s13415-013-0205-3.

Merten, J. (2005). Culture, gender and the recognition of the basic emotions. *Psychologia, 48*(4), 306–316. https://doi.org/10.2117/PSYSOC.2005.306.

Milton, D. E. (2012). The double empathy problem. *Disability & Society, 27*(6), 883–887.

Mischkowski, D., Crocker, J., & Way, B. M. (2016). From painkiller to empathy killer: Acetaminophen (paracetamol) reduces empathy for pain. *Social Cognitive and Affective Neuroscience, 11*(9), 1345–1353. https://doi.org/10.1093/scan/nsw057.

Mishor, E., Amir, D., Weiss, T., et al. (2021). Sniffing the human body volatile hexadecanal blocks aggression in men but triggers aggression in women. *Science Advances, 7*(47), 1–11. https://doi.org/10.1126/SCIADV.ABG1530.

Moore, A., Gorodnitsky, I., & Pineda, J. (2012). EEG mu component responses to viewing emotional faces. *Behavioural Brain Research, 226*(1), 309–316. https://doi.org/10.1016/J.BBR.2011.07.048.

Morawska, A. (2020). The effects of gendered parenting on child development outcomes: A systematic review. *Clinical Child and Family Psychology Review, 23*(4), 553–576. https://doi.org/10.1007/S10567-020-00321-5.

Morelli, S. A., Sacchet, M. D., & Zaki, J. (2015). Common and distinct neural correlates of personal and vicarious reward: A quantitative meta-analysis. *NeuroImage, 112*, 244–253. https://doi.org/10.1016/j.neuroimage.2014.12.056.

Morrison, I., Lloyd, D., di Pellegrino, G., & Roberts, N. (2004). Vicarious responses to pain in anterior cingulate cortex: Is empathy a multisensory issue. *Cognitive, Affective, & Behavioral Neuroscience, 4*(2), 270–278.

Mukamel, R., Ekstrom, A. D., Kaplan, J., Iacoboni, M., & Fried, I. (2010). Single-neuron responses in humans during execution and observation of actions. *Current Biology, 20*(8), 750–756. https://doi.org/10.1016/J.CUB.2010.02.045.

Murphy, B. A., & Lilienfeld, S. O. (2019). Are self-report cognitive empathy ratings valid proxies for cognitive empathy ability? Negligible meta-analytic relations with behavioral task performance. *Psychological Assessment, 31*(8), 1062–1072. https://doi.org/10.1037/pas0000732.

Murphy, B. A., Lilienfeld, S. O., & Algoe, S. B. (2022). Why we should reject the restrictive isomorphic matching definition of empathy. *Emotion Review, 14*(3), 167–181.

Naor, N., Shamay-Tsoory, S. G., Sheppes, G., & Okon-Singer, H. (2017). The impact of empathy and reappraisal on emotional intensity recognition.

Cognition and Emotion, 32(5), 972–987. https://doi.org/10.1080/02699931
.2017.1372366.

Naor, N., Shamay-Tsoory, S. G., Sheppes, G., & Okon-Singer, H. (2018). The
impact of empathy and reappraisal on emotional intensity recognition.
Cognition and Emotion, 32(5), 972–987.

Nath, S., Marie, A., Ellershaw, S., Korot, E., & Keane, P. A. (2022). New
meaning for NLP: the trials and tribulations of natural language processing
with GPT-3 in ophthalmology. *British Journal of Ophthalmology, 106*(7),
889–892. https://doi.org/10.1136/BJOPHTHALMOL-2022-321141.

Neumann, D. L., Chan, R. C. K., Boyle, G. J., Wang, Y., & Westbury, H. R.
(2015). Measures of empathy: Self-report, behavioral, and neuroscientific
approaches. In G. J. Boyle, D. H. Saklofske, & G. Matthews (Eds.), *Measures
of Personality and Social Psychological Constructs*. Elsevier, pp. 257–289.
https://doi.org/10.1016/B978-0-12-386915-9.00010-3.

Neumann, D. L., & Westbury, H. R. (2011). The psychophysiological measurement of empathy. In D. J. Scapaletti (Ed.), *Psychology of Empathy*. Nova
Science, pp. 119–142.

Nisbett, R. E., Choi, I., Peng, K., & Norenzayan, A. (2001). Culture and systems
of thought: Holistic versus analytic cognition. *Psychological Review, 108*(2),
291–310. https://doi.org/10.1037/0033-295X.108.2.291.

Noy, L., Dekel, E., & Alon, U. (2011). The mirror game as a paradigm for
studying the dynamics of two people improvising motion together.
*Proceedings of the National Academy of Sciences of the United States of
America, 108*(52), 20947–20952. https://doi.org/10.1073/PNAS.11081
55108.

Nummenmaa, L., Glerean, E., Viinikainen, M., et al. (2012). Emotions promote
social interaction by synchronizing brain activity across individuals.
*Proceedings of the National Academy of Sciences of the United States of
America, 109*(24), 9599–9604. https://doi.org/10.1073/PNAS.1206095109.

Ong, D. C. (2021). An ethical framework for guiding the development of
affectively-aware artificial intelligence. *2021 9th International Conference
on Affective Computing and Intelligent Interaction, ACII*. https://doi.org/
10.1109/ACII52823.2021.9597441.

Ong, D. C., Zaki, J., & Goodman, N. D. (2019). Computational models of
emotion inference in theory of mind: A review and roadmap. *Topics in
Cognitive Science, 11*(2), 338–357. https://doi.org/10.1111/TOPS.12371.

Orm, S., Vatne, T., Tomeny, T. S., & Fjermestad, K. (2022). Empathy and
prosocial behavior in siblings of children with autism spectrum disorder:
A systematic review. *Review Journal of Autism and Developmental
Disorders, 9*(2), 235–248. https://doi.org/10.1007/S40489-021-00251-0.

Osborne-Crowley, K. (2020). Social cognition in the real world: Reconnecting the study of social cognition with social reality. *Review of General Psychology*, *24*(2), 144–158. https://doi.org/10.1177/1089268020906483.

Palomba, D., Sarlo, M., Angrilli, A., Mini, A., & Stegagno, L. (2000). Cardiac responses associated with affective processing of unpleasant film stimuli. *International Journal of Psychophysiology*, *36*(1), 45–57. https://doi.org/10.1016/S0167-8760(99)00099-9.

Palumbo, R. V., Marraccini, M. E., Weyandt, L. L., et al. (2017). Interpersonal autonomic physiology: A systematic review of the literature. *Personality and Social Psychology Review*, *21*(2), 99–141. https://doi.org/10.1177/1088868316628405.

Paradiso, E., Gazzola, V., & Keysers, C. (2021). Neural mechanisms necessary for empathy-related phenomena across species. *Current Opinion in Neurobiology*, *68*, 107–115. https://doi.org/10.1016/j.conb.2021.02.005.

Patel, S., Scherer, K. R., Björkner, E., & Sundberg, J. (2011). Mapping emotions into acoustic space: The role of voice production. *Biological Psychology*, *87*(1), 93–98. https://doi.org/10.1016/J.BIOPSYCHO.2011.02.010.

Paulus, F. M., Müller-Pinzler, L., Stolz, D. S., et al. (2018). Laugh or cringe? Common and distinct processes of reward-based schadenfreude and empathy-based fremdscham. *Neuropsychologia*, *116*, 52–60. https://doi.org/10.1016/j.neuropsychologia.2017.05.030.

Pellicano, E., & den Houting, J. (2022). Annual research review: Shifting from 'normal science' to neurodiversity in autism science. *Journal of Child Psychology and Psychiatry*, *63*(4), 381–396.

Peng, W., Lou, W., Huang, X., et al. (2021). Suffer together, bond together: Brain-to-brain synchronization and mutual affective empathy when sharing painful experiences. *NeuroImage*, *238*, 1–11. https://doi.org/10.1016/j.neuroimage.2021.118249.

Perenc, L., & Pęczkowski, R. (2018). Cognitive and affective empathy among adolescent siblings of children with a physical disability. *Disability and Health Journal*, *11*(1), 43–48. https://doi.org/10.1016/J.DHJO.2017.08.008.

Pérez-Edgar, K., MacNeill, L. A., & Fu, X. (2020). Navigating through the experienced environment: Insights from mobile eye tracking. *Current Directions in Psychological Science*, *29*(3), 286–292. https://doi.org/10.1177/0963721420915880.

Perry, A., Bentin, S., Bartal, I. B. A., Lamm, C., & Decety, J. (2010). "Feeling" the pain of those who are different from us: Modulation of EEG in the mu/alpha range. *Cognitive, Affective and Behavioral Neuroscience*, *10*(4), 493–504. https://doi.org/10.3758/CABN.10.4.493.

Perry, A., Saunders, S. N., Stiso, J., et al. (2017). Effects of prefrontal cortex damage on emotion understanding: EEG and behavioural evidence. *Brain, 140*(4), 1086–1099. https://doi.org/10.1093/brain/awx031.

Pineda, J. A. (2005). The functional significance of mu rhythms: Translating "seeing" and "hearing" into "doing." *Brain Research Reviews, 50*(1), 57–68. https://doi.org/10.1016/J.BRAINRESREV.2005.04.005.

Pineda, J. A., & Hecht, E. (2009). Mirroring and mu rhythm involvement in social cognition: Are there dissociable subcomponents of theory of mind? *Biological Psychology, 80*(3), 306–314. https://doi.org/10.1016/J.BIOPSYCHO .2008.11.003.

Pinti, P., Tachtsidis, I., Hamilton, A., et al. (2020). The present and future use of functional near-infrared spectroscopy (fNIRS) for cognitive neuroscience. *Annals of the New York Academy of Sciences, 1464*(1), 5–29. https://doi.org/ 10.1111/NYAS.13948.

Pittelkow, M. M., aan het Rot, M., Seidel, L. J., Feyel, N., & Roest, A. M. (2021). Social anxiety and empathy: A systematic review and meta-analysis. *Journal of Anxiety Disorders, 78*,1–16. https://doi.org/10.1016/J.JANXDIS .2021.102357.

Ponnet, K., Buysse, A., Roeyers, H., & de Clercq, A. (2008). Mind-reading in young adults with ASD: Does structure matter? *Journal of Autism and Developmental Disorders, 38*(5), 905–918. https://doi.org/10.1007/S10803-007-0462-5.

Ponnet, K., Buysse, A., Roeyers, H., & de Corte, K. (2005). Empathic accuracy in adults with a pervasive developmental disorder during an unstructured conversation with a typically developing stranger. *Journal of Autism and Developmental Disorders, 35*(5), 585–600. https://doi.org/10.1007/S10803-005-0003-Z.

Ponnet, K. S., Roeyers, H., Buysse, A., de Clercq, A., & van der Heyden, E. (2004). Advanced mind-reading in adults with Asperger syndrome. *Autism, 8* (3), 249–266. https://doi.org/10.1177/1362361304045214.

Powell, P. A. (2018). Individual differences in emotion regulation moderate the associations between empathy and affective distress. *Motivation and Emotion, 42*(4), 602–613. https://doi.org/10.1007/s11031-018-9684-4.

Preckel, K., Kanske, P., & Singer, T. (2018). On the interaction of social affect and cognition: empathy, compassion and theory of mind. *Current Opinion in Behavioral Sciences, 19*, 1–6. https://doi.org/10.1016/j.cobeha.2017 .07.010.

Prehn-Kristensen, A., Wiesner, C., Bergmann, T. O., Wolff, S., & Jansen, O. (2009). Induction of empathy by the smell of anxiety. *PLoS ONE, 4*(6), 1–9. https://doi.org/10.1371/journal.pone.0005987.

Preis, M. A., & Kroener-Herwig, B. (2012). Empathy for pain: The effects of prior experience and sex. *European Journal of Pain (United Kingdom)*, *16*(9), 1311–1319. https://doi.org/10.1002/j.1532-2149.2012.00119.x.

Preis, M. A., Schmidt-Samoa, C., Dechent, P., & Kroener-Herwig, B. (2013). The effects of prior pain experience on neural correlates of empathy for pain: An fMRI study. *Pain*, *154*(3), 411–418. https://doi.org/10.1016/j.pain.2012.11.014.

Preston, S. D., & de Waal, F. B. M. (2002). Empathy: Its ultimate and proximate bases. *Behavioral and Brain Sciences*, *25*(1), 1–72.

Quintana, P., Nolet, K., Baus, O., & Bouchard, S. (2019). The effect of exposure to fear-related body odorants on anxiety and interpersonal trust toward a virtual character. *Chemical Senses*, *44*(9), 683–692. https://doi.org/10.1093/chemse/bjz063.

Rainville, P., Duncan, G. H., Price, D. D., Carrier, B., & Bushnell, M. C. (1997). Pain affect encoded in human anterior cingulate but not somatosensory cortex. *Science*, *277*(5328), 968–971. https://doi.org/10.1126/SCIENCE.277.5328.968.

Ravreby, I., Snitz, K., & Sobel, N. (2022). There is chemistry in social chemistry. *Science Advances*, *8*(25), 1–11. https://doi.org/10.1126/SCIADV.ABN0154.

Ren, Q., Lu, X., Zhao, Q., Zhang, H., & Hu, L. (2020). Can self-pain sensitivity quantify empathy for others' pain? *Psychophysiology*, *57*(10), 1–16. https://doi.org/10.1111/psyp.13637.

Ren, Q., Yang, Y., Wo, Y., Lu, X., & Hu, L. (2022). Different priming effects of empathy on neural processing associated with firsthand pain and nonpain perception. *Annals of the New York Academy of Sciences*, *1509*(1), 184–202. https://doi.org/10.1111/nyas.14723.

Riečanský, I., & Lamm, C. (2019). The role of sensorimotor processes in pain empathy. *Brain Topography*, *32*(6), 965–976. https://doi.org/10.1007/s10548-019-00738-4.

Rocha, M., Parma, V., Lundström, J. N., & Soares, S. C. (2018). Anxiety body odors as context for dynamic faces: Categorization and psychophysiological biases. *Perception*, *47*(10–11), 1054–1069. https://doi.org/10.1177/0301006618797227.

Rodríguez-Hidalgo, C., Tan, E. S. H., & Verlegh, P. W. J. (2017). Expressing emotions in blogs: The role of textual paralinguistic cues in online venting and social sharing posts. *Computers in Human Behavior*, *73*, 638–649. https://doi.org/10.1016/J.CHB.2017.04.007.

Roeyers, H., Buysse, A., Ponnet, K., & Pichal, B. (2001). Advancing advanced mind-reading tests: Empathic accuracy in adults with a pervasive developmental disorder. *Journal of Child Psychology and Psychiatry, 42*(2), 271–278. https://doi.org/10.1111/1469-7610.00718.

Rueda, P., Fernández-Berrocal, P., & Baron-Cohen, S. (2014). Dissociation between cognitive and affective empathy in youth with Asperger syndrome. *European Journal of Developmental Psychology, 12*(1), 85–98. https://doi.org/10.1080/17405629.2014.950221.

Rum, Y., Genzer, S., Markovitch, N., Jenkins, J., Perry, A., & Knafo-Noam, A. (2022). Are there positive effects of having a sibling with special needs? Empathy and prosociality of twins of children with non-typical development. *Child Development, 93*(4), 1121–1128. https://doi.org/10.1111/CDEV.13740.

Rum, Y., & Perry, A. (2020). Empathic accuracy in clinical populations. *Frontiers in Psychiatry, 11*, 1–23. https://doi.org/10.3389/FPSYT.2020.00457.

Rütgen, M., Seidel, E. M., Pletti, C., et al. (2018). Psychopharmacological modulation of event-related potentials suggests that first-hand pain and empathy for pain rely on similar opioidergic processes. *Neuropsychologia, 116*, 5–14. https://doi.org/10.1016/j.neuropsychologia.2017.04.023.

Rütgen, M., Seidel, E. M., Riečanský, I., & Lamm, C. (2015). Reduction of empathy for pain by placebo analgesia suggests functional equivalence of empathy and first-hand emotion experience. *Journal of Neuroscience, 35* (23), 8938–8947. https://doi.org/10.1523/JNEUROSCI.3936-14.2015.

Rütgen, M., Seidel, E. M., Silani, G., et al. (2015). Placebo analgesia and its opioidergic regulation suggest that empathy for pain is grounded in self pain. *Proceedings of the National Academy of Sciences of the United States of America, 112*(41), E5638–E5646. https://doi.org/10.1073/pnas.1511269112.

Saarela, M. V., Hlushchuk, Y., Williams, A. C. D. C., et al. (2007). The compassionate brain: Humans detect intensity of pain from another's face. *Cerebral Cortex, 17*(1), 230–237. https://doi.org/10.1093/cercor/bhj141.

Sasson, N. J., Pinkham, A. E., Richard, J., et al. (2010). Controlling for response biases clarifies sex and age differences in facial affect recognition. *Journal of Nonverbal Behavior, 34*(4), 207–221. https://doi.org/10.1007/S10919-010-0092-Z.

Sato, W., Fujimura, T., & Suzuki, N. (2008). Enhanced facial EMG activity in response to dynamic facial expressions. *International Journal of Psychophysiology, 70*(1), 70–74. https://doi.org/10.1016/J.IJPSYCHO.2008.06.001.

Sauter, D. A., Eisner, F., Calder, A. J., & Scott, S. K. (2010). Perceptual cues in nonverbal vocal expressions of emotion. *Quarterly Journal of Experimental Psychology, 63*(11), 2251–2272. https://doi.org/10.1080/1747021100 3721642.

Sauter, D. A., Eisner, F., Ekman, P., & Scott, S. K. (2010). Cross-cultural recognition of basic emotions through nonverbal emotional vocalizations. *Proceedings of the National Academy of Sciences of the United States of America, 107*(6), 2408–2412. https://doi.org/10.1073/PNAS.0908239106.

Sauter, D. A., Eisner, F., Ekman, P., & Scott, S. K. (2015). Emotional vocalizations are recognized across cultures regardless of the valence of distractors. *Psychological Science, 26*(3), 354–356. https://doi.org/10.1177/095679761 4560771.

Schilbach, L., Timmermans, B., Reddy, V., et al. (2013). Toward a second-person neuroscience. *Behavioral and Brain Sciences, 36*(4), 393–414. https://doi.org/10.1017/S0140525X12000660.

Schurz, M., Radua, J., Tholen, M. G., et al. (2021). Toward a hierarchical model of social cognition: A neuroimaging meta-analysis and integrative review of empathy and theory of mind. *Psychological Bulletin, 147*(3), 293–327. https://doi.org/10.1037/bul0000303.

Schwartz-Ziv, R., & Tishby, N. (2017). Opening the black box of deep neural networks via information. *ArXiv Preprint ArXiv:1703.00810.* https://doi.org/ 10.48550/arxiv.1703.00810

Sened, H., Bar-Kalifa, E., Pshedetzky-Shochat, R., Gleason, M., & Rafaeli, E. (2020). Fast and slow empathic perceptions in couples' daily lives use different cues. *Affective Science, 1*(2), 87–96.

Sened, H., Lavidor, M., Lazarus, G., et al. (2017). Empathic accuracy and relationship satisfaction: A meta-analytic review. *Journal of Family Psychology, 31*(6), 742–752. https://doi.org/10.1037/FAM0000320.

Shamay-Tsoory, S. G., Shur, S., Barcai-Goodman, L., et al. (2007). Dissociation of cognitive from affective components of theory of mind in schizophrenia. *Psychiatry Research, 149*(1–3), 11–23. https://doi.org/10.1016/J .PSYCHRES.2005.10.018.

Sheng, F., Liu, Q., Li, H., Fang, F., & Han, S. (2014). Task modulations of racial bias in neural responses to others' suffering. *NeuroImage, 88*, 263–270. https://doi.org/10.1016/J.NEUROIMAGE.2013.10.017.

Sherman, J. W., Klauer, K. C., & Allen, T. J. (2021). *Mathematical Modeling of Implicit Social Cognition: The Machine in the Ghost*. In B. Gawronski & B. K. Payne (Eds.), *Handbook of implicit social cognition: Measurement, theory, and applications*. The Guilford Press, pp. 156–174

Shipp, S. (2016). Neural elements for predictive coding. *Frontiers in Psychology, 7*, 1–21. https://doi.org/10.3389/FPSYG.2016.01792/ BIBTEX.

Shvimmer, S., Simhon, R., Gilad, M., & Yitzhaky, Y. (2022). Classification of emotional states via transdermal cardiovascular spatiotemporal facial patterns using multispectral face videos. *Scientific Reports*, *12*(1), 1–16. https://doi.org/10.1038/s41598-022-14808-4.

Singer, T., & Klimecki, O. M. (2014). Empathy and compassion. *Current Biology*, *24*(18), R875–R878. https://doi.org/10.1016/J.CUB.2014.06.054.

Singer, T., & Lamm, C. (2009). The social neuroscience of empathy. *Annals of the New York Academy of Sciences*, *1156*, 81–96. https://doi.org/10.1111/j.1749-6632.2009.04418.x.

Singer, T., Seymour, B., O'Doherty, J., et al. (2004). Empathy for pain involves the affective but not sensory components of pain. *Science*, *303*(5661), 1157–1162. https://doi.org/10.1126/science.1094645.

Singer, T., Seymour, B., O'Doherty, J. P. (2006). Empathic neural responses are modulated by the perceived fairness of others. *Nature*, *439*(7075), 466–469. https://doi.org/10.1038/nature04271.

Smith, M. J., Horan, W. P., Karpouzian, T. M., et al. (2012). Self-reported empathy deficits are uniquely associated with poor functioning in schizophrenia. *Schizophrenia Research*, *137*(1–3), 196–202. https://doi.org/10.1016/J.SCHRES.2012.01.012.

Soto, J. A., & Levenson, R. W. (2009). Emotion recognition across cultures: The influence of ethnicity on empathic accuracy and physiological linkage. *Emotion*, *9*(6), 874–884. https://doi.org/10.1037/A0017399.

Spies, M., Hahn, A., Kranz, G. S., et al. (2016). Gender transition affects neural correlates of empathy: A resting state functional connectivity study with ultra high-field 7T MR imaging. *Neuroimage*, *138*, 257–265.

Spreng, R. N., McKinnon, M. C., Mar, R. A., & Levine, B. (2009). The Toronto empathy questionnaire: Scale development and initial validation of a factor-analytic solution to multiple empathy measures. *Journal of Personality Assessment*, *91*(1), 62–71. https://doi.org/10.1080/0022389080 2484381.

Stellar, J. E., Manzo, V. M., Kraus, M. W., & Keltner, D. (2012). Class and compassion: Socioeconomic factors predict responses to suffering. *Emotion*, *12*(3), 449–459.

Stephens, G. J., Silbert, L. J., & Hasson, U. (2010). Speaker-listener neural coupling underlies successful communication. *Proceedings of the National Academy of Sciences of the United States of America*, *107*(32), 14425–14430. https://doi.org/10.1073/pnas.1008662107.

Stinson, L., & Ickes, W. (1992). Empathic accuracy in the interactions of male friends versus male strangers. *Journal of Personality and Social Psychology*, *62*(5), 787–797. https://doi.org/10.1037/0022-3514.62.5.787.

Sundberg, J., Patel, S., Björkner, E., & Scherer, K. R. (2011). Interdependencies among voice source parameters in emotional speech. *IEEE Transactions* on *Affective Computing*, *2*(3), 162–174. https://doi.org/10.1109/T-AFFC.2011.14.

Suzuki, Y., Galli, L., Ikeda, A., Itakura, S., & Kitazaki, M. (2015). Measuring empathy for human and robot hand pain using electroencephalography. *Scientific Reports*, *5*, 1–9. https://doi.org/10.1038/srep15924.

Tandon, R., Gaebel, W., Barch, D. M., et al. (2013). Definition and description of schizophrenia in the DSM-5. *Schizophrenia Research*, *150*(1), 3–10. https://doi.org/10.1016/J.SCHRES.2013.05.028.

Tempesta, D., Socci, V., de Gennaro, L., & Ferrara, M. (2018). Sleep and emotional processing. *Sleep Medicine Reviews*, *40*, 183–195. https://doi.org/10.1016/J.SMRV.2017.12.005.

Thomas, G., & Fletcher, G. J. O. (2003). Mind-reading accuracy in intimate relationships: Assessing the roles of the relationship, the target, and the judge. *Journal of Personality and Social Psychology*, *85*(6), 1079–1094. https://doi.org/10.1037/0022-3514.85.6.1079.

Thomas, G., & Maio, G. R. (2008). Man, I feel like a woman: When and how gender-role motivation helps mind-reading. *Journal of Personality and Social Psychology*, *95*(5), 1165–1179. https://doi.org/10.1037/A0013067.

Thompson, A., Bartholomeusz, C., & Yung, A. R. (2011). Social cognition deficits and the "ultra high risk" for psychosis population: A review of literature. *Early Intervention in Psychiatry*, *5*(3), 192–202. https://doi.org/10.1111/J.1751-7893.2011.00275.X.

Thompson, A. E., & Voyer, D. (2014). Sex differences in the ability to recognise non-verbal displays of emotion: A meta-analysis. *Cognition and Emotion*, *28*(7), 1164–1195. https://doi.org/10.1080/02699931.2013.875889.

Thompson, A., Papas, A., Bartholomeusz, C., et al. (2012). Social cognition in clinical "at risk" for psychosis and first episode psychosis populations. *Schizophrenia Research*, *141*(2–3), 204–209. https://doi.org/10.1016/J.SCHRES.2012.08.007.

Timmers, I., Park, A. L., Fischer, M. D., et al. (2018). Is empathy for pain unique in its neural correlates? A meta-analysis of neuroimaging studies of empathy. *Frontiers in Behavioral Neuroscience*, *12*, 1–12. https://doi.org/10.3389/fnbeh.2018.00289.

Timmons, A. C., Margolin, G., & Saxbe, D. E. (2015). Physiological linkage in couples and its implications for individual and interpersonal functioning: A literature review. *Journal of Family Psychology*, *29*(5), 720–731. https://doi.org/10.1037/fam0000115.

Trilla, I., Weigand, A., & Dziobek, I. (2021). Affective states influence emotion perception: Evidence for emotional egocentricity. *Psychological Research*, *85*(3), 1005–1015. https://doi.org/10.1007/S00426-020-01314-3.

Tzafilkou, K., Economides, A. A., & Protogeros, N. (2021). Mobile sensing for emotion recognition in smartphones: A literature review on non-intrusive methodologies. *International Journal of Human–Computer Interaction, 38*(11), 1037–1051.

Uljarevic, M., & Hamilton, A. (2013). Recognition of emotions in autism: A formal meta-analysis. *Journal of Autism and Developmental Disorders, 43*(7), 1517–1526. https://doi.org/10.1007/S10803-012-1695-5.

Uzefovsky, F., & Knafo-Noam, A. (2016). Empathy development throughout the life span. In J. A. Sommerville & J. Decety (Eds.), *Social Cognition Development across the Life Span.* Routledge, pp. 89–115. https://doi.org/10.4324/9781315520575-12.

Viessmann, O., & Polimeni, J. R. (2021). High-resolution fMRI at 7 Tesla: Challenges, promises and recent developments for individual-focused fMRI studies. *Current Opinion in Behavioral Sciences, 40*, 96–104. https://doi.org/10.1016/J.COBEHA.2021.01.011.

Vishne, G., Jacoby, N., Malinovitch, T., Epstein, T., & Ahissar, M. (2021). Slow update of internal representations impedes synchronization in autism. *Nature Communications, 12*(1), 1–15. https://doi.org/10.1038/s41467-021-25740-y.

Vollberg, M. C., & Cikara, M. (2018). The neuroscience of intergroup emotion. *Current Opinion in Psychology, 24*, 48–52. https://doi.org/10.1016/J.COPSYC.2018.05.003.

Wang, M. Y., Luan, P., Zhang, J., Xiang, Y. T., Niu, H., & Yuan, Z. (2018). Concurrent mapping of brain activation from multiple subjects during social interaction by hyperscanning: A mini-review. *Quantitative Imaging in Medicine and Surgery, 8*(8), 819–837. https://doi.org/10.21037/QIMS.2018.09.07.

Wang, Y., Song, W., Tao, W., et al. (2022). A systematic review on affective computing: Emotion models, databases, and recent advances. *Information Fusion, 83–84*, 19–52. https://doi.org/10.1016/J.INFFUS.2022.03.009,

Watt, D. (2014). Toward a neuroscience of empathy: Integrating affective and cognitive perspectives. *Neuropsychoanalysis, 9*(2), 146–151. https://doi.org/10.1080/15294145.2007.10773550.

Weisz, E., & Zaki, J. (2017). Empathy building interventions: A review of existing work and suggestions for future directions. In E. Seppala, E. Simon-Thomas, S.L. Brown et al. (Eds.), *The Oxford Handbook of Compassion Science.* Oxford University Press, pp. 205–217.

Weisz, E., & Zaki, J. (2018). Motivated empathy: A social neuroscience perspective. *Current Opinion in Psychology, 24*, 67–71. https://doi.org/10.1016/j.copsyc.2018.05.005.

Wells, J. L., Haase, C. M., Rothwell, E. S., et al. (2022). Positivity resonance in long-term married couples: Multimodal characteristics and consequences for health and longevity. *Journal of Personality and Social Psychology, 123*(5), 983–1003. https://doi.org/10.1037/PSPI0000385.

Wheatley, T., Boncz, A., Toni, I., & Stolk, A. (2019). Beyond the isolated brain: The promise and challenge of interacting minds. *Neuron, 103*(2), 186–188. https://doi.org/10.1016/J.NEURON.2019.05.009.

Whitehouse, A. J., Hickey, M., & Ronald, A. (2011). Are autistic traits in the general population stable across development?. *PLoS ONE, 6*(8), 1–8.

Wicker, B., Keysers, C., Plailly, J., Royet, J.-P., Gallese, V., & Rizzolatti, G. (2003). Both of us disgusted in my insula: The common neural basis of seeing and feeling disgust. *Neuron, 40*, 655–664.

Williams, A. C. D. C. (2002). Facial expression of pain: An evolutionary account. *Behavioral and Brain Sciences, 25*(4), 439–455. https://doi.org/10.1017/S0140525X02000080.

Wu, T., & Han, S. (2021). Neural mechanisms of modulations of empathy and altruism by beliefs of others' pain. *ELife, 10*, 1–36. https://doi.org/10.7554/eLife.66043.

Xiao, B., Can, D., Georgio, P. G., Atkins, D., & Natayanan, S. S. (2012). Analyzing the language of therapist empathy in motivational interview based psychotherapy. In *Proceedings of the 2012 Asia Pacific Signal and Information Processing Association Annual Summit and Conference*, 1–4. https://ieeexplore.ieee.org/abstract/document/6411762.

Xiao, B., Imel, Z. E., Georgiou, P., Atkins, D. C., & Narayanan, S. S. (2016). Computational analysis and simulation of empathic behaviors: A survey of empathy modeling with behavioral signal processing framework. *Current Psychiatry Reports, 18*, 1–11.

Xygkou, A., Siriaraya, P., Covaci, A., et al. (2023). The "conversation" about loss: Understanding how chatbot technology was used in supporting people in grief. In *Proceedings of the 2023 CHI Conference on Human Factors in Computing Systems*.

Yitzhak, N., Pertzov, Y., Guy, N., & Aviezer, H. (2020). Many ways to see your feelings: Successful facial expression recognition occurs with diverse patterns of fixation distributions. *Emotion, 22*(5), 844–860. https://doi.org/10.1037/EMO0000812.

Yoon, S., Byun, S., & Jung, K. (2018). Multimodal speech emotion recognition using audio and text. *2018 IEEE Spoken Language Technology Workshop (SLT)*, 112–118. https://doi.org/10.1109/SLT.2018.8639583.

Young, G. W., O'Dwyer, N., & Smolic, A. (2021). Exploring virtual reality for quality immersive empathy building experiences. *Behaviour and*

Information Technology, *41*(16), 3415–3431. https://doi.org/10.1080/0144929X.2021.1993336.

Zaki, J. (2014). Empathy: A motivated account. *Psychological Bulletin, 140*(6), 1608–1647. https://doi.org/10.1037/a0037679.

Zaki, J., Bolger, N., & Ochsner, K. (2008). It takes two the interpersonal nature of empathic accuracy. *Psychological Science, 19*(4), 399–404.

Zaki, J., & Ochsner, K. (2012). The neuroscience of empathy: Progress, pitfalls and promise. *Nature Neuroscience, 15*(5), 675–680. https://doi.org/10.1038/nn.3085.

Zaki, J., & Ochsner, K. (2011). Reintegrating the study of accuracy into social cognition research. *Psychological Inquiry, 22*(3), 159–182. https://doi.org/10.1080/1047840X.2011.551743.

Zaki, J., Wager, T. D., Singer, T., Keysers, C., & Gazzola, V. (2016). The anatomy of suffering: Understanding the relationship between nociceptive and empathic pain. *Trends in Cognitive Sciences, 20*(4), 249–259. https://doi.org/10.1016/j.tics.2016.02.003.

Zaki, J., Weber, J., Bolger, N., & Ochsner, K. (2009). The neural bases of empathic accuracy. *Proceedings of the National Academy of Sciences, 106*(27), 11382–11387. www.pnas.orgcgidoi10.1073pnas.0902666106.

Zhao, Q., Neumann, D. L., Yan, C., Djekic, S., & Shum, D. H. (2021). Culture, sex, and group-bias in trait and state empathy. *Frontiers in Psychology, 12*, 1–19.

Zheng, L., Wang, Q., Cheng, X., et al. (2016). Perceived reputation of others modulates empathic neural responses. *Experimental Brain Research, 234*(1), 125–132. https://doi.org/10.1007/s00221-015-4434-2.

Zheng, L., Zhang, F., Wei, C., et al. (2016). Decreased empathic responses to the "lucky guy" in love: The effect of intrasexual competition. *Frontiers in Psychology, 7*, 1–8. https://doi.org/10.3389/fpsyg.2016.00660.

Zhou, Q., Valiente, C., & Eisenberg, N. (2004). Empathy and its measurement. In S. J. Lopez & C. R. Snyder (Eds.), *Positive Psychological Assessment: A Handbook of Models and Measures*. American Psychological Association, pp. 269–284. https://doi.org/10.1037/10612-017.

Zhou, Z. H. (2021). Machine learning. In *Machine Learning*. Springer Nature, pp. 1–23. https://doi.org/10.1007/978-981-15-1967-3_8.

Cambridge Elements ☰

Perception

James T. Enns
The University of British Columbia

Editor James T. Enns is Professor at the University of British Columbia, where he researches the interaction of perception, attention, emotion, and social factors. He has previously been Editor of the *Journal of Experimental Psychology: Human Perception and Performance* and an Associate Editor at *Psychological Science, Consciousness and Cognition, Attention Perception & Psychophysics,* and *Visual Cognition.*

About the Series
The modern study of human perception includes event perception, bidirectional influences between perception and action, music, language, the integration of the senses, human action observation, and the important roles of emotion, motivation, and social factors. Each Element in the series combines authoritative literature reviews of foundational topics with forward-looking presentations of the recent developments on a given topic.

Cambridge Elements ⹀

Perception

Elements in the Series

A full series listing is available at: www.cambridge.org/EPER

Printed in the United States
by Baker & Taylor Publisher Services